W9-CFB-950

BISTRO CHICKEN

BROADWAY BOOKS

BISTRO CHICKEN

100 Easy Yet Elegant Recipes with French Flair

✳

MARY ELLEN EVANS

PRINTED IN CHINA

BROADWAY BOOKS and its logo, a letter B bisected on the diagonal, are trademarks of Random House, Inc.

Visit our website at www.broadwaybooks.com

Book design by Dina Dell'Arciprete Houser/dk Design Partners, Inc.
Illustrated by Sophie Allport

Library of Congress Cataloging-in-Publication Data

Evans, Mary Ellen, 1948–
    Bistro chicken : 100 easy yet elegant recipes with French flair / Mary Ellen Evans.
        p. cm.
    Includes index.
    (pbk. : alk. paper)
    1. Cookery (Chicken) 2. Cookery, French. I. Title.
TX750.5.C45E94 2004
641.6'65—dc21   2003051801

ISBN 0-7679-1378-7

10 9 8 7 6 5 4 3 2 1

ACKNOWLEDGMENTS

Thanks go to my editor, Jennifer Josephy, and my agent, Stacey Glick, for their input on this book.

My husband, Glen, deserves huge thanks for his endless support throughout this book and for washing many a skillet and Dutch oven. My children, Melanie and Eric, and my best friends, Hallie, Raghavan, and Sena, deserve my gratitude for listening when I needed an ear and for handing out gentle pep talks when I needed a boost.

I also want to thank my Sunday supper group for cheerfully serving as informal tasters and testers, eating and preparing chicken recipes for over a year.

CONTENTS

INTRODUCTION

Jet-lagged and longing for a decent meal, I stumble each time from the plane in Paris and think "roast chicken." Drawing sustenance from that thought, I make my way into the city, unpack, and anticipate the perfect traveler's meal.

Zigzagging in and out of fatigue, I make my way down narrow streets lined with pastry shops and shoe stores, refusing to be distracted from the promised land of bistro dining. Ignoring the cute black high-heeled shoes arranged so enticingly in one of the windows, I remind myself that right now what I need is food. After a journey of airline pap consumed in a seat designed for a hobbit, my top priority is real nourishment in a welcoming atmosphere.

I turn the corner, and, with the Eiffel Tower peeking around the bend, suddenly I'm there—"there" being any one of a number of establishments in the seventh arrondissement, the quarter I call home on my frequent visits to this city of lights. The window-lined exterior, framed with wood paneling, proclaims "bistro" better than any neon sign. In case I have any doubts, the figured lace curtains hung halfway down the glass panes document its authenticity. The name of this mecca is almost immaterial; a bistro's very nature guarantees certain menu items. Poulet rôti is one.

And so, after the requisite exchange of greetings, I am seated on my bentwood chair at my small table, which is draped with a cloth and, depending on the caliber of the establishment, another smaller cloth or a protective square of butcher paper. After ordering a kir for an aperitif and then my dinner, I sit back and prepare to be revived. Soon the perfect solace to mind and body arrives, my succulent quarter chicken, richly brown and gleaming against its white plate. Without extra frills and accompanied almost always with *pommes frites* (French fries), this ritual reacquaintance with the joys of ordinary food prepared extraordinarily well is a kick-off to further pleasurable dining to come.

In the days that follow, as the journey expands beyond Paris throughout the French countryside or to my small house in Provence, those pleasurable dining experiences often include other equally delightful poultry-based meals, for in France as well as here, chicken is truly a versatile ingredient. Small restaurants, brasseries, and even corner cafés sauté, simmer, and stew this most humble bird into some of the most satisfying eating experiences available.

Bistro meals come together quickly and, with most of the labor done earlier in the day, arrive at the table from oven or pot in little time and with little effort. Many tiny French restaurants are staffed by husband and wife teams. One works the kitchen and one the front of the house, taking orders and serving customers. The kitchen is most often a tiny place, sometimes the size of a closet. Rapidly prepared food is a requirement, so dishes either enter and exit the skillet in short order or lend themselves to a simple rewarming.

Hence the rationale for *Bistro Chicken*. The bistro style adapts well to home cooking. Whether for a weekday meal or a casual company dinner, the recipes that follow offer easy solutions with an elegant feel. This book features honest food, without the pretension of the more elaborate, labor-intensive *haute cuisine* of a three-star restaurant, while upholding the French passion for the best possible results.

Affordable and readily available, chicken adapts to a range of treatments, from whole to cut up, fryers to stewing hens, breasts to thighs, boneless to bone-in, and everything in between, including the egg. The recipes explore the wide range of culinary treatments available. Each one includes a *truc,* or trick, with tips that clarify the cooking process. They draw their inspiration from Paris to the Caribbean and the various *départements* of France, each one equally passionate about its own regional cuisine.

With this book as a guide, my French roast chicken can be yours at home, along with ninety-nine other possibilities for enjoying the warmly satisfying experience of bistro eating.

A Chicken Primer

ot all chickens are created equal. Some seem blessed with far more taste than others; some are also more expensive. Often the two go hand in hand.

Let's start with the basic supermarket bird. Bred under less than ideal conditions, the industrial chicken is serviceable at best. Crowded together throughout a brief life span in large houses with flooring covered by litter, these chickens consume feed containing antibiotics to prevent infection and promote rapid growth. While economical, they are often exceedingly bland when cooked.

From there, we head into the morass of terms used to describe other breeding conditions. The first, and most vague, is "natural." This description indicates that the processing plant uses no antibiotics but does not guarantee what the chicken received earlier in its life. "Free range" indicates access to the outdoors but it still pays to know your supplier. The access might be to a small concrete run and nothing more. These birds tend to be a bit larger in size and their flesh a bit firmer. Certified organic establishes a documented procedure for raising poultry according to specific standards, an organic feed of grains and soybeans, and a specific method of slaughter. Generally speaking, birds with any of these titles often have more flavor than those with a mass-market upbringing.

Chickens come to market very quickly. The following describes the various types found in today's marketplace.

* The most frequently sold poultry falls under the category of broiler/fryer. Most sources put these chickens at 2.8 to about 4.5 pounds, dressed and ready for sale, with a life span of 6 to 8 weeks.

* Roasters are similar to fryers except larger, 4.75 to 7 pounds, taking a bit longer to come to market, 8 to 12 weeks. Sometimes older birds are marketed as roasters and can be tough.

* Capons are castrated roosters with plump and moist flesh because of their high fat content. They range from 4 to 10 pounds, with the majority weighing in at 6 to 9 pounds. They typically live to about 15 weeks but can be older.

* Stewing chickens, categorized as hens by the USDA, are older, tougher birds that require long, slow cooking. They vary in weight, are most often heavier because of their age, usually 5 or 6 pounds, and are generally 10 to 12 months old.

* Rock Cornish game hens are small chickens, weighing 1½ to 2 pounds and only up to 6 weeks old. They are a cross between a Cornish chicken and a White Rock chicken.

* Also available through certain sources are poussins, or squab chickens—not squabs, which are pigeons—that are truly tiny, weighing in at about a pound at 4 to 6 weeks of age.

Chickens are graded by the USDA and labeled A, B, or C, in descending order of quality. Only buy Grade A.

My personal preference is for a vegetable-fed bird; a vegetarian diet tends to guarantee an excellent flavor. When I can, I shop from favorite suppliers at local farmers' markets but, for the most part, for time and convenience, I pick up my chicken at the nearest supermarket. Many now offer a range of possibilities and provide excellent choices. The recipes in this book are based on commonly available sizes for whole birds or parts and will work with any type of chicken, from mass produced to organic.

The term *breast* in this book refers to the most common usage, which is half of the whole breast section.

Some general cooking techniques are important. Since chicken, and meat in general, will not brown when wet, make sure to pat all surfaces dry with a paper towel before seasoning. Don't crowd the pieces when sautéing or the meat will steam and stay pale instead of browning. The proteins in chicken, particularly breasts, do not take well to boiling, which results in tough meat. Check stovetop sautés, simmers, and stews to make sure they don't cook too vigorously. Investing in a glass cover makes this easy to do.

The titles in this book use French terms for chicken that require a brief explanation.

* *Blancs de volaille* or *blancs de poulet,* in most French recipes, generally mean boneless chicken breasts. In this book, the breasts are also skinless, since this is the way they appear in American markets.

* *Chapon* translates as capon.

* *Coq* stands for a mature rooster but, based on what's available in the usual market, the recipes in this book designate weight, not sex or age.

* *Cuisse* is the French term for the drumstick / thigh portion. When I order my poulet rôti in France, I ask for the cuisse because I'm partial to the moistness of dark meat.

* *Oeufs* is the French word for eggs. It is pronounced "ough," as in one egg is enough.

* *Poule* can refer to a specific method of raising a female chicken, sometimes called a *poularde,* or, more generally, to a larger chicken cooked with moist heat, such as a *poule au pot.*

* *Poulet* is used here to refer to chickens in the broiler/fryer category. It literally translates as chicken.

* *Suprêmes,* a term sometimes translated to mean a boneless breast cut, is used in France to indicate a chicken breast, on the bone, with a portion of wing attached. I use it here to indicate bone-in breast pieces, which are marketed in this country without the wing.

* *Volaille* means poultry and, in France, is a category that includes game birds and rabbit.

Should you have the rare good fortune to do some cooking in France, keep in mind that the French have their share of mediocre poultry, too. Look for a chicken marked with the designation *Label Rouge,* meeting strict standards for feeding and raising, or, if possible, a *poulet de Bresse,* the near legendary, flavorful free-range chickens that are raised in the Burgundy region. Bresse chickens have an *appellation d'origine contrôlée*— an AOC—which is only given to quality products, mostly wines, from a specifically defined area, and which is highly regulated.

Finally, most of the dishes in this book require only simple accompaniments. Some have specific serving suggestions, but many need only rice or potatoes on the side, a basket of crusty bread, and a simple salad before or after to enable you to duplicate the bistro experience. Add a glass of wine and good conversation and the recipe for successful dining is complete.

PETITS PLATS DE POULET

Appetizer, Luncheon, and First Course Dishes

AILERONS DE VOLAILLE AU PAPRIKA

PAPRIKA WINGS

In the past few years, Spanish and Latin American culture has become a new craze in Paris and beyond. Close to Place de la Bastille, bodegas and small restaurants offer tapas and paella along with pulsing salsa music and a nightclub atmosphere. Even in Provence, I found evidence of the far-reaching effects of this trend. After a morning of successful shopping at Vaison-la-Romaine's Tuesday market, I needed a little sustenance before returning to my house in nearby Mollans. It seemed as though all of my fellow shoppers had the same idea and were rapidly filling the outdoor tables in the cafés ringing the market square. One of the busiest featured an extensive collection of tapas, little nibbles that included these wings—exactly what I needed before driving home with my market treasures.

Some markets sell the meatiest portions of the wing, pre-cut, under the name of "chicken drummies." Using these saves the time of trimming the whole wing into segments; buy eighteen "drummie" pieces.

MAKES 6 SERVINGS

⅓ cup yogurt

2 tablespoons sweet Spanish or
   Hungarian paprika

2 tablespoons red wine

2 teaspoons minced garlic

1½ teaspoons sherry vinegar

½ teaspoon salt

⅛ teaspoon cayenne

9 whole chicken wings or 18 drummies

2 tablespoons cornstarch

✳

TRUC:

TRY THESE WITH A SMOKED SWEET SPANISH
PAPRIKA FOR AN EXTRA DIMENSION OF FLAVOR.

Preheat the oven to 425°F. Line a shallow
15 × 10-inch baking pan with parchment paper.

Mix the yogurt, paprika, red wine, garlic,
sherry vinegar, salt, and cayenne together in
a medium bowl. Remove the wing tips from
the chicken wings; reserve in the freezer for
stock. Cut each wing into two pieces at the
remaining joint; add to the yogurt mixture.
Stir thoroughly to coat. Sprinkle with
cornstarch; stir again to blend and coat.

Place the wings in a single layer in the prepared
pan. Bake for 30 to 35 minutes, until richly
browned and the tops are crisp. Remove and
serve hot or at room temperature.

CHICKEN BROTH

When time allows, making chicken broth is one of the more satisfying, easy, and truly rewarding occupations in the kitchen. The actual effort is minimal and the slow-cooked aroma of a barely simmering soup pot is almost its own reward. In bistro kitchens, large kettles filled with extra chicken parts and trimmings gently bubble on back burners in time-honored tradition. Served with crunchy, toasted slices of leftover bread and dusted with freshly grated Parmesan, this warming broth is food for the soul as well as the body.

MAKES 10 CUPS BOUILLON

3½ to 4 pounds chicken pieces and scraps,
  including parts of a stewing hen

2 medium carrots, quartered

1 large onion, quartered

1 large celery stalk with leafy top, quartered

1 medium leek, white and pale green portions
  only, quartered and thoroughly rinsed

6 sprigs parsley

4 sprigs thyme

1 bay leaf

6 peppercorns

1½ teaspoons salt

Croutons (croutes; see Note)

Freshly grated Parmigiano-Reggiano cheese

Rinse the chicken thoroughly to remove any trapped blood. Place in a large stockpot and cover with 3½ quarts of cold water. Bring just to a boil over medium-high heat, 10 to 15 minutes. Reduce the heat to medium-low to maintain a simmer; simmer for 10 minutes. Skim to remove any surface foam; add the vegetables, herbs, and seasonings. Reduce the heat to low; cook, partially covered, for 2½ hours, adjusting the heat as necessary so that the surface is broken only by occasional bubbles. Strain through several layers of cheesecloth.

Refrigerate the bouillon overnight; remove the surface fat.

To serve, allowing about 1 cup per person, bring the quantity desired to a simmer over medium-low heat. Serve in bowls. Top with a crouton and about 1 tablespoon Parmesan per bowl.

Note: To make the croutons (*croutes*), slice stale French bread into ½-inch-thick slices. Arrange in a single layer on a shallow baking sheet; brush lightly with olive oil. Rub the surface of one side with a crushed clove of garlic. Toast in a 400°F oven for 6 to 8 minutes, until crisp.

TRUCS:

WHEN PREPARING OTHER RECIPES, SAVE CHICKEN SCRAPS IN A LARGE, SELF-SEALING PLASTIC BAG IN YOUR FREEZER. PARTS OF CARCASSES, WING TIPS, NECKS, GIZZARDS, AND HEARTS CAN ALL BE ADDED. SAVE THE LIVERS SEPARATELY FOR ANOTHER USE; THEIR FLAVOR IS TOO STRONG FOR BROTHS AND STOCKS. DO MAKE SURE TO ADD SOME ACTUAL CHICKEN PIECES FOR A REAL CHICKEN TASTE. FOR THE BEST FLAVOR USE STEWING HEN PARTS, SOMETIMES STOCKED IN THE FREEZER SECTION OF THE MEAT DEPARTMENT IN YOUR GROCERY STORE.

ONCE MADE, THIS BROTH CAN ALSO BE USED IN ANY OF THE RECIPES CALLING FOR CANNED, REDUCED-SODIUM CHICKEN BROTH. MAKE A BATCH, OMITTING THE CROUTONS AND PARMESAN, AND FREEZE IT IN 1- OR 2-CUP PORTIONS FOR LATER USE.

MOROCCAN PHYLLO RECTANGLES

I first stumbled across these crunchy, savory pastries as a luncheon item in a small restaurant called 7ème Sud in Paris. They served them on lovely North African plates with a simple tomato and cucumber salad on the side. Their name comes from the traditional wrapping used to hold them together. Both Tunisians and Moroccans use a paper-thin round of dough, called a brik, as a casing for various fillings. Phyllo is a readily available substitute in this country.

MAKES 4 SERVINGS

½ teaspoon mild curry powder

¼ teaspoon ground ginger

¼ teaspoon salt

⅛ teaspoon cinnamon

⅛ teaspoon ground coriander

Pinch cayenne

½ cup olive oil (approximately)

1 medium onion, chopped (about ¾ cup)

½ cup chopped cooked new or fingerling potatoes

1 cup chopped cooked chicken

2 large eggs

Eight 17 × 12-inch leaves phyllo

Preheat the oven to 400°F. Combine the curry powder, ginger, salt, cinnamon, coriander, and cayenne; set aside.

Heat 2 tablespoons of the olive oil in a medium skillet over medium heat. When hot, add the onion. Sauté until the onion begins to soften, 3 to 4 minutes. Add the potatoes and cook for an additional 3 minutes. Add the chicken and sprinkle with the spice mixture; stir to blend. Whisk the eggs until foamy; pour over the mixture in the skillet. Cook, stirring frequently, until the eggs are set, 1 to 2 minutes; remove from the heat.

Brush one sheet of phyllo with a light coating of olive oil. Fold in half to form a 12 × 8½-inch rectangle. Brush lightly with oil and fold in half again to form a 6 × 8½-inch rectangle. Brush lightly with oil again. Form a 4 × 1½-inch rectangle of the chicken mixture in the center of the phyllo rectangle; fold the two shorter sides over the filling, so that they meet in the middle. Fold the remaining two sides over the filling and each other. Brush lightly with oil; turn over and place on an ungreased baking sheet. Brush the top lightly with oil. Repeat with the remaining sheets of phyllo. Bake for 10 to 12 minutes, until golden brown. Serve.

TRUCS:

THESE CAN BE MADE AHEAD AND FROZEN. TO SERVE, JUST ARRANGE THEM ON A BAKING SHEET, STILL FROZEN, AND REHEAT THEM FOR 10 TO 15 MINUTES IN A 375°F OVEN. TO SEE IF THE FILLING IS WARM, PIERCE THE CENTER OF ONE OF THE BRIKS WITH THE TIP OF A THIN KNIFE AND LEAVE IT THERE BRIEFLY. THEN PLACE THE SIDE OF THE KNIFE TIP AGAINST THE BACK OF YOUR WRIST; IF THE TIP IS WARM, SO IS THE FILLING.

WITH HEAT, THE SPECIAL FLAVOR OF EXTRA VIRGIN OLIVE OIL DISSIPATES, SO IT'S FINE TO USE REGULAR OLIVE OIL INSTEAD. SAVE THE HIGHER-QUALITY, EXTRA VIRGIN OIL FOR VINAIGRETTES OR WHEN EXPOSURE TO HIGHER TEMPERATURES IS LIMITED.

CRÊPES AU POULET ET CÈPES

CHICKEN AND PORCINI-FILLED CRÊPES

Crêpe sellers are scattered on street corners throughout Paris, preparing one of the few French food items sold for consumption on the go. Most of their offerings are sweet; my personal favorite is spread with Nutella and topped with sliced banana. These lacy thin pancakes make wonderful wrappers for savory fillings as well, especially this combination of chicken, mushrooms, and cheese. Small restaurants serve items like this in individual, boat-shaped ramekins that hold two plump crêpes and their sauce perfectly.

MAKES 6 FIRST COURSE OR LUNCHEON SERVINGS OR 4 MAIN COURSE SERVINGS

CRÊPES

1 cup sparkling water

¾ cup milk

2 large eggs

2 tablespoons canola oil

1½ cups all-purpose flour

⅛ teaspoon salt

FILLING AND TOPPING

2 cups reduced-sodium chicken broth

½ ounce dried porcini mushrooms (cèpes)

5 tablespoons butter

1 tablespoon canola oil

¼ cup minced shallots

8 ounces white button mushrooms, sliced

2 cups diced cooked chicken

½ teaspoon salt

¼ teaspoon freshly ground pepper

5 tablespoons all-purpose flour

¾ cup white wine

¼ cup heavy cream

4 ounces grated Emmentaler or Gruyère cheese
   (about 1 cup)

For the crêpes, put ¾ cup of the sparkling water, the milk, eggs, and canola oil in a blender; pulse to blend. Add the flour and salt; pulse to blend. Let the batter rest for 15 minutes; stir in the remaining ¼ cup of sparkling water.

Heat a 7-inch crêpe pan over medium heat. When hot, wipe with a paper towel dipped in canola oil. Ladle in a scant ¼ cup of the batter; swirl to thinly coat the bottom and sides of the crêpe pan. Cook until the edges of the crêpe start to pull away from the pan and the crêpe is browned, 30 to 45 seconds. Carefully flip with a spatula; cook for an additional 10 to 15 seconds. Slide onto a plate; repeat with the remaining batter to form 12 crêpes, separating each with paper towels. Set aside.

Meanwhile, for the filling and sauce, heat ½ cup of the broth in a small saucepan over low heat until simmering, 3 to 4 minutes. Add the dried mushrooms; remove from the heat and let steep until softened, about 30 minutes. Remove the mushrooms; reserve the mushroom liquid. Coarsely chop the mushrooms and set aside. Strain the mushroom liquid through a fine strainer lined with a paper towel; set aside.

Preheat the oven to 425°F. Heat 1 tablespoon of the butter and the canola oil in a large skillet over medium-high heat. When sizzling, add the shallots; cook until beginning to soften, 1 to 2 minutes. Add the button mushrooms; cook until beginning to soften, 3 to 4 minutes. Add the reserved mushrooms and mushroom liquid;

reduce the heat to medium-low. Cook until all the liquid has evaporated, 5 to 8 minutes. Remove from the heat; stir in the chicken, salt, and pepper.

Heat the remaining 4 tablespoons of butter in a saucepan over medium heat. When melted, stir in the flour; stir to form a paste (roux). Cook to remove any floury taste, 1 to 2 minutes; whisk in the remaining 1½ cups of chicken broth and the white wine. Bring to a boil, scraping the bottom of the pan to make sure no roux is caught around the edges and whisking several times until smooth and lump free. Bring to a boil; boil until thickened, 3 to 4 minutes. Reserve 1 cup of the sauce; pour the remainder into the chicken and mushroom mixture. Stir the heavy cream into the reserved sauce.

Fill the crêpes with the chicken mixture, placing a spoonful of the mixture in the center of each crêpe and rolling it up. Place in six individual oval serving ramekins or in a shallow baking dish. Pour the remaining sauce over the center of the crêpes; top with the cheese. Bake for 10 minutes or until hot and bubbling. Serve.

✳

TRUC:

USING CARBONATED BEVERAGES WHEN MAKING A THIN BATTER IMPROVES THE TEXTURE. BESIDES SPARKLING WATER, TRY SPARKLING CIDER, BEER, OR EVEN LEFTOVER CHAMPAGNE FOR DIFFERENT FLAVOR POSSIBILITIES.

CROQUE MONSIEUR AU POULET

Croque Monsieur
Sandwich with Chicken

As a college student in Paris on a limited budget, I would sometimes treat myself to a purchased lunch, preferably a croque monsieur sandwich. The buttery crisp outside encased meltingly soft cheese plus a slice of meat—either ham or chicken—and was well worth the inexpensive splurge of eating out. In America, we often call the poultry version a croque madame but, for the French, the title of madame instead of monsieur indicates the sandwich comes topped with an egg. No matter what you call it, you'll be glad you tried this café classic.

MAKES 4 SERVINGS

4 ounces grated Emmentaler or Gruyère cheese
  (about 1 cup)
1 teaspoon all-purpose flour
¼ cup heavy cream
1 teaspoon Dijon mustard
1 teaspoon Cognac, optional
8 slices firm white bread
2 tablespoons butter
4 slices cooked chicken

Toss the cheese and flour together in a small bowl. Stir together the heavy cream, mustard, and Cognac, if using. Stir the cream mixture into the cheese mixture to form a paste.

Spread one side of each of the bread slices with butter; turn 4 slices over and spread with the cream-cheese mixture. Top with the chicken, then with the remaining bread slices, buttered side up.

Place the sandwiches in a large skillet; cover. Place the skillet over medium-low heat and cook until the sandwiches are nicely toasted, about 5 minutes. Turn the sandwiches over; cover and toast the other side, 3 to 4 minutes. Cut each sandwich in half to serve.

✳

TRUC:

SOMETIMES A CROQUE MONSIEUR INCLUDES *BÉCHAMEL,* OR WHITE SAUCE. BY BLENDING THE CHEESE WITH CREAM AND FLOUR, YOU MAKE SANDWICHES THAT CONVEY THE SAME VELVETY QUALITY WITH MUCH LESS EFFORT. TRY THESE WITH THE MORE COMMONLY USED HAM OR TURKEY, CORNED BEEF, OR PASTRAMI INSTEAD OF CHICKEN.

FLAN WITH CHICKEN LIVERS

True bistro food is not about the choicest tidbits but rather earthy ingredients prepared with care. In my opinion, chicken livers never had it so good as in this flan. Like the proverbial sow's ear and silk purse, a bit of cream, a splash of Madeira, and a few eggs transform these humble livers into the silkiest of creations.

MAKES 6 SERVINGS

½ pound chicken livers

½ teaspoon chopped garlic

1¼ cups heavy cream

¼ cup plus 2 tablespoons Madeira

3 large eggs

2 large egg yolks

2 tablespoons all-purpose flour

½ teaspoon salt

⅛ teaspoon freshly ground pepper

Pinch nutmeg

1 cup milk

2 tablespoons tomato paste

1½ tablespoons coarsely chopped fresh
   tarragon leaves

Preheat the oven to 350°F. Heavily butter six 6-ounce custard cups or six 4-ounce French timbale molds and place in a shallow baking pan. Put the chicken livers and garlic in a blender; add ¼ cup of the heavy cream and the 2 tablespoons of Madeira; purée. Add the eggs and egg yolks, flour, salt, pepper, and nutmeg; pulse to blend, scraping down the sides as necessary. Add the milk; pulse to blend. Pour into the prepared cups or molds (the custard cups should be about two-thirds full; the timbale molds should be filled to the top). Pour boiling water to a depth of ½ inch into the shallow baking pan. Bake for about 20 minutes or until puffed and a knife inserted in the center comes out clean. Invert onto small plates.

TRUCS:

When choosing chicken livers, look for firm, evenly colored lobes and avoid any that are dull and brown-tinged.

Adding the fresh tarragon at the very end ensures the brightest of tastes. It's normally a good idea to add fresh herbs toward the end of the cooking time to preserve their essence.

Meanwhile, just before removing the flans from the oven, place the remaining 1 cup of cream, the remaining ¼ cup of Madeira, and the tomato paste in a saucepan. Bring to a boil over medium-high heat; boil until reduced slightly, 4 to 5 minutes. Add the tarragon; spoon over the unmolded flans and serve.

PÂTÉ DE FOIES DE VOLAILLE
CHICKEN LIVER PÂTÉ

While eating foie gras on warm toast is my idea of heaven, this down-to-earth combination of lots of butter, shallots, and the best chicken livers available is a more approachable (and affordable) substitute. This pâté is another French classic that deserves status in the culinary hall of fame.

MAKES 2 CUPS

½ pound (2 sticks) salted butter

⅓ cup chopped shallots

1 pound chicken livers

2 tablespoons Cognac

½ cup reduced-sodium chicken broth

1½ teaspoons fresh thyme leaves

½ teaspoon salt

⅛ teaspoon freshly ground pepper

Heat 1 stick of the butter in a large skillet over medium heat until melted. Add the shallots; sauté for 1 minute. Add the chicken livers; sauté, turning occasionally, until just barely pink in the center, 8 to 10 minutes. Pour the Cognac over the livers. Immediately light with a match to flame, cooking until the flames disappear and the livers are cooked through. Remove from the heat; stir in the broth, thyme, salt, and pepper. Let cool to room temperature, about 20 minutes.

Put the mixture in the bowl of a food processor fitted with a metal blade; process until puréed. Add the remaining stick of butter, cut in pieces; process until smooth. Pour into a 2-cup crock; chill, covered, for 5 to 6 hours or up to 3 days.

TRUC:

RECIPES CALL FOR FLAMING FOR SEVERAL
REASONS. IN DISHES SUCH AS CRÊPES
SUZETTE, THE FIRE IS MOSTLY FOR SHOW.
IN RECIPES SUCH AS THIS ONE, THE COGNAC IS
IGNITED FOR TWO REASONS. ONE IS TO
QUICKLY BURN OFF MOST OF THE ALCOHOL
WITHOUT OVERCOOKING THE CHICKEN LIVERS;
THE SECOND IS TO SEAL THE FLAVOR OF THE
COGNAC INTO THE LIVERS.

les herbes

les herbes

CHICKEN PIZZA

*E*very time I return to the French countryside, there seem to be even more pizzerias. The locals have their choice of sit-down, restaurantlike settings or take-out from one of the many pizza trucks that frequent small towns and villages. Our own village of Mollans is no exception. The wonderful aroma of the wood-burning stove from the small pizza parlor on the edge of town mingles in the most pleasant way with the vapors from the lavender factory nearby. On Fridays, our choice expands when the pizza truck pulls up next to the bridge and sells precooked delights from the side window. This particular recipe is an adaptation from an offering in the nearby town of Buis-les-Baronnies.

MAKES TWO 14-INCH PIZZAS

Cornmeal for sprinkling

3 cups unbleached all-purpose flour

One ¼-ounce package of quick-rising yeast

1 tablespoon sugar

1 teaspoon salt

1 tablespoon extra virgin olive oil

1 cup corn kernels (fresh or frozen and thawed)

1 cup diced cooked boiling or fingerling potatoes

⅔ cup diced red onions

1 tablespoon herbes de Provence

1½ teaspoons minced garlic

⅔ cup tomato sauce

6 ounces shredded Emmentaler or Gruyère cheese
   (about 1½ cups)

4 ounces shredded mozzarella cheese
   (about 1 cup)

2 cups diced cooked chicken

½ cup coarsely chopped pitted Nyons or
   kalamata olives

Place the oven racks in the middle and lower third of the oven. Preheat the oven to 450°F. Lightly grease two pizza pans or cookie sheets; sprinkle them lightly with cornmeal.

Stir together 2½ cups of the flour, the yeast, sugar, and ¾ teaspoon of the salt in a medium bowl. Add the olive oil to 1 cup of moderately warm water (115°F); stir into the flour mixture to form a soft dough. Sprinkle the counter with a small amount of the remaining flour. Turn out the dough onto the floured counter; knead, adding small amounts of flour as necessary to prevent sticking, until the dough is resilient and barely sticky. Cover and let rise for 15 minutes.

Meanwhile, toss the corn, potatoes, red onions, herbes de Provence, garlic, and remaining ¼ teaspoon of salt in a medium bowl; set aside. When the dough has risen, cut in two and gently shape into balls, working the dough as

little as possible. Sprinkle the counter with any remaining flour or a small amount of additional flour as necessary. Roll each ball into a disk slightly larger than the pizza pan (the dough will shrink when lifted). Place on the prepared pans. Spread each with ⅓ cup of the tomato sauce to form a very thin layer. Sprinkle each with half of the vegetable mixture. Bake for 5 minutes, staggering the pans' location in the oven so one pizza is not directly above the other. (Rotate one pizza from the middle to the lower rack and the other from the lower rack to the middle.) Bake for an additional 5 minutes. Remove from the oven. Sprinkle each with the cheeses; top with the chicken and olives. Return to the oven and bake for 4 to 6 minutes, until the crust is a rich deep brown. (Remove the bottom pizza first; let the top pizza cook an additional minute or two.) Serve.

TRUC:

MY FAVORITE QUICK-RISING YEAST IS, OF COURSE, FRENCH. THE BRAND NAME IS SAF AND, ALTHOUGH A BIT MORE EXPENSIVE THAN OTHERS, IT PRODUCES EXCELLENT RESULTS.

CHICKEN RILLETTES

*S*ay "rillettes" *(pronounced ree-yet) to any Frenchman and he will know what you mean, while most Americans haven't a clue. That's unfortunate because this tasty spread is a great, economical appetizer that requires very little effort. Most often made with pork, it can be made with duck, salmon, or chicken, as here. As an added bonus when you're entertaining, it benefits from being made in advance. Serve it with thinly sliced bread as an appetizer or as a spread for sandwiches.*

MAKES 1¾ CUPS

4 bone-in, skin-on chicken thighs

1 small onion, halved

2 cloves

1 teaspoon dried thyme

Large pinch allspice

1 bay leaf

⅓ cup reduced-sodium chicken broth

1 tablespoon Cognac

¼ teaspoon salt

Place the chicken thighs in the bottom of a 4½-quart slow cooker. Pierce each onion half with a clove; add to the slow cooker. Sprinkle with ½ teaspoon of the thyme, allspice, and the bay leaf. Pour the broth and Cognac over all. Cover and cook on the low setting until the chicken falls from the bone when lifted from the cooker, 8 to 9 hours. Remove the chicken; let cool briefly. Discard the onion halves and bay leaf; strain the cooking liquid.

When the chicken is cool enough to handle, remove the skin and bones; place the chicken in a medium bowl. Using two forks, shred the chicken. Slowly stir in the cooking juices with a fork, creating finer and finer shreds until all the liquid is incorporated and the chicken has a slightly fluffy texture. Season with the remaining ½ teaspoon of thyme and the salt. Pack into a decorative crock; refrigerate, covered, overnight for the flavors to blend.

✳

TRUCS:

A SLOW COOKER STREAMLINES COOKING THE THIGHS UNTIL THE MEAT IS FALLING OFF THE BONE. JUST POP THE INGREDIENTS INTO THE POTTERY CROCK IN THE MORNING AND, WITHOUT FURTHER TENDING, EVERYTHING IS PROPERLY COOKED BY EVENING.

DON'T BE TEMPTED TO USE CHICKEN BREASTS OR BONELESS, SKINLESS THIGHS FOR THIS RECIPE. THE LONG COOKING REQUIRES DENSE THIGH PORTIONS WHOSE SKIN ADDS THE FAT NECESSARY FOR A PROPER, SPREADABLE TEXTURE AT THE END. IN ADDITION, BOTH THE SKIN AND THE BONES ADD AN EXTRA BOOST OF CHICKEN FLAVOR.

Curried Chicken Salad Sampler

While walking down the street in Paris on a sunny September day, I realized the lunch hour was rapidly disappearing and that suddenly I was starving. Finding myself in an area where I had no favorite restaurant nearby and too famished to change locations, I started looking for a café with lots of customers, usually a sign the food is good. Surprisingly, the busiest place was a chain restaurant, called Au Poivron. The food proved to be solid if not inspired. With some tinkering, I've adapted their salad idea into something quite pleasing.

MAKES 4 SERVINGS

CHUTNEY POTATO SALAD

3 medium Yukon Gold potatoes, quartered
   (about ¾ pound)
1 tablespoon cider vinegar
1 tablespoon mango chutney
1½ teaspoons whole seed mustard
½ teaspoon salt
¼ teaspoon freshly ground pepper
¼ cup canola oil
2 tablespoons chopped green onions
⅓ cup raisins

CURRIED CHICKEN SALAD

½ cup mayonnaise
3 tablespoons imported hazelnut oil
2 tablespoons chopped shallots

1 tablespoon mild curry powder
¼ teaspoon salt
2 cups diced cooked chicken

CUCUMBER SALAD

2 medium cucumbers, peeled, seeded, and diced
½ cup nonfat yogurt
½ teaspoon cumin seeds
¼ teaspoon salt

6 cups torn leaf lettuce
2 small tomatoes, cut into 6 wedges each
4 slices nut bread, toasted, buttered,
   and quartered

For the chutney potato salad, cook the potatoes in salted water to cover in a saucepan over medium-high heat until just tender, 25 to 30 minutes. Drain; let cool briefly.

Meanwhile, whisk together the cider vinegar, chutney, mustard, salt, and pepper. Slowly whisk in the canola oil. Add the green onions. When the potatoes are cool enough to handle, cut into ½-inch dice; add to the bowl along with the raisins. Toss to coat. Let cool to room temperature or refrigerate, covered, until ready to serve.

For the curried chicken salad, whisk together the mayonnaise and hazelnut oil until emulsified. Whisk in the shallots, curry powder, and salt. Add the chicken; stir to coat.

For the cucumber salad, combine the cucumbers, yogurt, cumin seeds, and salt in a medium bowl.

When ready to serve, divide the lettuce among four plates. Place one-fourth of the potato salad in a mound on each plate, slightly off center. Repeat with the chicken salad and cucumber salad. Garnish each salad with 3 tomato wedges and 4 bread quarters and serve.

TRUC:

MAKE LARGER BATCHES OF EACH OF THE SALADS AND SERVE THEM BUFFET STYLE FOR A WEDDING OR BABY SHOWER ALONG WITH A FRESH FRUIT PLATE. BUY CRUSTY WALNUT ROLLS FROM YOUR FAVORITE BAKERY ALONG WITH THEIR BEST DESSERT AND YOUR MENU IS COMPLETE.

CHICKEN, CORN, AND TOMATO SALAD

During the summer in Paris, cafés and bistros spill their tables practically to the street, taking advantage of the fine weather. Customers are in a good mood and, over lunch, the atmosphere amid the din and bustle is almost partylike. Often the selections are chalked on a board and the mainstay is salads. This one, with its seasonal ingredients, is among the most popular.

MAKES 4 SERVINGS

3 tablespoons tarragon wine vinegar

1 large shallot, chopped (about 3 tablespoons)

2 teaspoons chopped fresh tarragon

1 teaspoon Dijon mustard

¼ teaspoon salt

⅛ teaspoon freshly ground pepper

½ cup canola oil

½ pound small red boiling potatoes

8 cups mixed greens

2 cups diced cooked chicken

1 cup cooked corn kernels

2 large tomatoes, cut into 8 wedges each

To make a vinaigrette, whisk the tarragon wine vinegar, shallot, tarragon, mustard, salt, and pepper together. Slowly whisk in the canola oil.

Cook the potatoes in salted water to cover in a saucepan over medium-high heat until tender, 25 to 30 minutes. Drain; cool to lukewarm. Cut into ¼-inch-thick slices; place in a small bowl. Toss with ¼ cup of the vinaigrette. Let marinate for 30 minutes or until ready to serve.

Divide the greens among four dinner plates. Place ½ cup chicken in the center of each plate. Arrange the potato slices, corn, and tomato wedges in a decorative pattern around the chicken. Drizzle with the remaining vinaigrette and serve.

TRUC:

ALTHOUGH THE CORN IN MOST SMALL PARISIAN RESTAURANTS IS USUALLY FROZEN OR SOMETIMES EVEN CANNED, WE HAVE THE LUXURY OF SUCCULENT FRESH EARS DURING THE HEIGHT OF SUMMER. TAKE TWO SMALLER EARS AND PLACE IN A MICROWAVE-SAFE CONTAINER WITH A LITTLE WATER. MICROWAVE ON HIGH UNTIL JUST BARELY DONE, 3 TO 4 MINUTES. LET COOL AND SHAVE THE KERNELS FROM THE COB. CORN COOKS BEAUTIFULLY IN THE MICROWAVE AND, FOR ONE OR TWO EARS, THIS METHOD IS MUCH FASTER THAN BRINGING WATER TO A BOIL FOR STOVETOP COOKING.

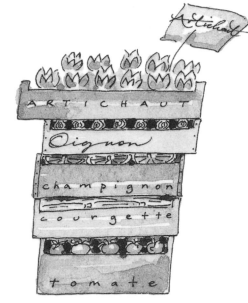

CHICKEN LIVERS ON GREENS WITH PAN JUICES

In Lyon, bistros are often called bouchons. These tiny restaurants often specialize in using ingredients from all the parts of an animal in the tastiest of ways. This dish is a Lyonnais favorite that I first tasted at Chez Hugon, seated at a smoky table near the bar. From this vantage, I watched the owner serve pots, the 46 cl. bottles of house wine typical of the region, to regulars and tourists alike to wash down the hearty fare.

MAKES 4 SERVINGS

10 cups torn escarole, curly endive, Swiss chard, spinach, or romaine leaves

8 chicken livers

½ teaspoon salt

¼ teaspoon freshly ground pepper

¼ cup canola oil

3 strips bacon

1 cup crusty bread in 1-inch cubes

2 teaspoons minced garlic

2 tablespoons red wine vinegar

Place the escarole in a large bowl. Cut the chicken livers in half. Pat dry; season with ¼ teaspoon of the salt and ⅛ teaspoon of the pepper.

Heat the canola oil in a large skillet over medium heat. When hot, add the bacon; fry until crisp. Drain on paper towels. Add the cubed bread; sauté until browned, turning frequently, 2 to 3 minutes. Remove; drain on paper towels. Add the chicken livers; sauté until just cooked through, 6 to 8 minutes. Remove the chicken livers to a small plate; remove the skillet from the heat.

Add the garlic to the hot oil remaining in the skillet; pour over the escarole. Add the red wine vinegar, the remaining ¼ teaspoon of salt, and the remaining ⅛ teaspoon of pepper to the hot skillet; scrape up any brown bits clinging to the bottom of the pan. Pour over the escarole; toss to coat with the oil and vinegar.

Divide the escarole among four plates; top with the croutons and chicken livers. Crumble the bacon over all and serve immediately.

✳

TRUC:

ADDING THE VINEGAR TO THE HOT SKILLET TEMPERS ITS ACIDIC TASTE WHILE REDUCING AND CONCENTRATING THE WINE-BASED FLAVOR. THAT'S WHY IT'S IMPORTANT TO USE THE BEST-QUALITY VINEGAR YOU CAN FIND. ASK LOCAL SPECIALTY SHOPS WHAT THEY CARRY AND ASK FOR RECOMMENDATIONS.

SMOKED TEA–POACHED CHICKEN

Mariage Frères is always on my to-do list whenever I am in Paris. There I stock up on my favorite teas. On busy days, the queue can be long but no one rushes. Every patron, once at the counter, is given a clerk's undivided attention; large tins are lowered from wooden shelves and proffered for smelling the delicate aromas. Once chosen, the selections are placed in sacks with care while the customer pays at the cashier and returns to pick up his or her waiting package. At the Left Bank branch, lunch is served on the second floor and the items often feature tea as an ingredient.

MAKES 4 SERVINGS

1 tablespoon Lapsang Souchong tea

1 tablespoon Earl Grey tea

Four 5-ounce boneless, skinless chicken breasts

12 to 16 plump asparagus spears, peeled
(about 1 pound)

3 tablespoons fresh lemon juice

1 tablespoon soy sauce

1½ teaspoons Dijon mustard

⅛ teaspoon freshly ground pepper

3 tablespoons canola oil

8 cups fresh greens

1 large orange or tangerine, peeled and segmented

Bring 3 cups of water to a boil in a medium saucepan over medium heat. Remove from the heat; add the teas. Let steep for 5 minutes. Strain; return the tea liquid to the saucepan. Bring to a simmer over medium-low heat; add the chicken. Poach until the chicken is no longer pink in the thickest portion when cut with a knife, 12 to 15 minutes. Remove the chicken from the poaching liquid; let cool. Reserve 1 tablespoon of the poaching liquid.

Meanwhile, cook the asparagus in simmering water in a skillet or a large shallow saucepan until tender, 8 to 10 minutes. Remove; let cool.

TRUC:

MARIAGE FRÈRES SELLS A TEA CALLED SMOKY EARL GREY THAT COMBINES THE CITRUSY BERGAMOT-FLAVORED NOTES OF EARL GREY WITH HINTS OF THE SMOKY AROMA AND TASTE STRONGLY PRESENT IN LAPSANG SOUCHONG. SINCE MARIAGE FRÈRES TEA ISN'T AS READILY AVAILABLE AS STARBUCKS COFFEE, STEEPING REGULAR LAPSANG SOUCHONG AND EARL GREY TOGETHER APPROXIMATES THE TASTE OF THE MARIAGE FRÈRES BLEND.

To make the vinaigrette, whisk together the lemon juice, soy sauce, reserved poaching liquid, mustard, and pepper. Slowly whisk in the canola oil.

Just before serving, toss the greens with ¼ cup of the vinaigrette; divide among four plates. Slice the chicken breasts on a diagonal; place each breast in a fan shape slightly off center on the greens. Arrange 3 to 4 asparagus spears in between the chicken slices. Divide the orange segments equally among the salads, placing along the bottom of the asparagus spears. Drizzle the remaining vinaigrette over the top of the chicken and asparagus and serve.

CHICKEN AND WATERCRESS SALAD

Visit a market in France and be astonished by the depth and seasonality of the selections. Watercress is a case in point; small bunches of peppery leaves vibrate with freshness and practically demand to be taken home for immediate use in a salad, sauce, or soup. This recipe obliges, teaming together the cress's bite with creamy goat cheese, sweet beets, and crunchy walnuts. Chicken ties it all together for a dish that's vivid in color as well as flavor.

MAKES 4 SERVINGS

Four 5-ounce boneless, skinless chicken breasts
4 teaspoons white wine vinegar
1 tablespoon minced shallots
2 teaspoons whole seed mustard
⅛ teaspoon salt
⅛ teaspoon pepper
⅓ cup canola oil
4 cups watercress leaves
4 cups torn leaf lettuce
1 cup diced beets
4 ounces mild goat cheese, crumbled
½ cup walnut halves
¼ cup chopped chives

Bring 3 cups of water to a simmer in a medium saucepan over medium heat. Reduce the heat to medium-low; add the chicken. Poach until the chicken is no longer pink in the thickest portion when cut with a knife, 12 to 15 minutes. Remove the chicken from the poaching liquid; let cool and dice.

To make the vinaigrette, whisk the white wine vinegar, shallots, mustard, salt, and pepper together. Slowly whisk in the canola oil.

Combine the watercress and leaf lettuce in a medium bowl. Toss with the vinaigrette. Divide among four plates. Mound the diced chicken in the center of each plate; ring with the beets, goat cheese, and walnuts. Sprinkle the chives over all. Serve immediately.

TRUCS:

IN FRANCE, COOKED BEETS ARE SOLD IN PLASTIC-WRAPPED PACKAGES IN ALMOST EVERY SUPERMARKET. HERE, CANNED BEETS ARE A PERFECTLY ACCEPTABLE SUBSTITUTION.

FEEL FREE TO USE LEFTOVER DICED CHICKEN INSTEAD OF POACHED CHICKEN BREASTS FOR A MORE RUSTIC BUT EQUALLY TASTY PRESENTATION.

CHICKEN, PEAR, ROQUEFORT, AND WALNUT SALAD

*M*any times Roquefort is wasted in a salad, used where a less expensive blue would do just as well. Not here. The assertive saltiness of this sheep's milk cheese pairs particularly well with the sweetness of the pears, and the chicken and walnuts add substance and depth.

MAKES 4 SERVINGS

2 tablespoons vinaigre de Banyuls

¼ teaspoon salt

Pinch freshly ground pepper

3 tablespoons imported walnut oil

2 cups diced cooked chicken

5 cups lightly packed torn red romaine
   lettuce leaves

2 ripe Bartlett pears

1 cup walnut pieces

¼ pound Roquefort, crumbled

To make the vinaigrette, whisk the vinaigre de Banyuls, salt, and pepper together. Slowly whisk in the walnut oil.

Toss the chicken with 1 tablespoon of the vinaigrette in a bowl. Toss the red romaine with the remaining vinaigrette in a medium bowl; divide among four plates. Mound ½ cup chicken in the center of each plate. Cut the pears in half; remove the cores. Slice each half into 6 wedges; arrange around the chicken. Sprinkle with the walnut pieces and the crumbled Roquefort. Serve immediately.

✳

TRUC:

VINAIGRE DE BANYULS IS MADE FROM BANYÙLS WINE, A FORTIFIED RED WINE FROM THE LANGUEDOC REGION OF FRANCE. ITS SWEETNESS AND LIGHT CHARACTER BLEND WELL WITH ROQUEFORT, WHICH TYPICALLY DOES NOT WORK WITH OTHER VINEGARS. IF YOU CAN'T FIND IT, SUBSTITUTE 1 TABLESPOON LEMON JUICE IN PLACE OF THE 2 TABLESPOONS VINEGAR CALLED FOR IN THE RECIPE.

CHICKEN, APPLE, HAZELNUT, AND FOURME D'AMBERT SALAD

*L*ike the Chicken, Pear, Roquefort, and Walnut Salad, this recipe combines the elements of fruit, cheese, and nuts, but with strikingly different results. Here the major players work as a study in contrasts, with each element successfully serving as a foil for the others.

Made from cow's milk in the Auvergne rather than from sheep's milk as is Roquefort in the Languedoc, Fourme d'Ambert is a blue cheese with a flavor quite different from the better known Roquefort's. It is significantly creamier and not as sharp but still bursting with taste. If it's unavailable, try for a Bleu d'Auvergne or a high-quality domestic Gorgonzola.

MAKES 4 SERVINGS

1 tablespoon sherry vinegar

⅛ teaspoon salt

3 tablespoons imported hazelnut oil

4 cups lightly packed torn leaf lettuce

2 small Belgian endives, cut into pieces

2 cups diced cooked chicken

2 apples, cored and cut into large dice

1 cup toasted, skinned, and coarsely chopped hazelnuts (see Note)

¼ pound Fourme d'Ambert cheese, crumbled

To make the vinaigrette, whisk the sherry vinegar and salt together; slowly whisk in the hazelnut oil.

Toss the lettuce and Belgian endives together in a medium bowl; divide among four plates. Mound ½ cup chicken in the center of each plate; ring with apples. Sprinkle with the hazelnuts and crumbled Fourme d'Ambert. Serve immediately.

Note: To toast the hazelnuts, place on a shallow baking sheet in a 350°F oven. Bake for 8 to 10 minutes, until lightly browned under the flaking skins and fragrant. Remove from the baking sheet; wrap in a towel. After about 5 minutes, rub the nuts together in the towel to remove most of the skins. Let cool.

✳

TRUC:

IMPORTED HAZELNUT OIL, TASTING LIKE THE TOASTED NUTS FROM WHICH IT IS PRESSED, IS A LUXURIOUS ADDITION TO SALADS. AS IT TURNS RANCID EASILY, KEEP IT REFRIGERATED FOR MAXIMUM SHELF LIFE. IF HARD TO FIND, INCREASE THE AMOUNT OF HAZELNUTS IN THE RECIPE TO 1½ CUPS AND USE CANOLA OIL INSTEAD.

CHICKEN SALAD
WITH GRAPE TENDRILS

*P*urchasing vrilles de vignes *is virtually impossible, even in France. Made from scratch in restaurant and home kitchens from the tendrils of grapevines, they are pickled like cornichons and used as a condiment in the Quercy—home to Cahors wine and Rocamadour cheese. Although I've made them from a friend's untreated grapevines, I recommend using very thinly sliced grape leaves.*

MAKES 4 SERVINGS

1 tablespoon white wine vinegar

1 teaspoon Dijon mustard

1¼ teaspoons salt

⅛ teaspoon freshly ground pepper

3 tablespoons imported walnut oil

1 large carrot, cut into 3-inch lengths

1 medium leek, white and pale green portions
only, halved and thoroughly rinsed

1 large celery stalk, cut into 3-inch lengths

½ small onion, halved

2 cloves

Two 6- to 8-ounce boneless, skinless
chicken breasts

2 chicken-apple sausages (about ¼ pound)

6 cups lightly packed spring mesclun mix or
mixed greens

12 to 16 vrilles de vignes or ¼ cup thin strips
(chiffonnade) of grape leaves, packed in brine
and rinsed

½ teaspoon coarsely crushed peppercorn mélange

To make the vinaigrette, whisk the white wine vinegar, mustard, ¼ teaspoon of the salt, and pepper together. Slowly whisk in the walnut oil; set aside.

Place the carrot, leek, and celery in a Dutch oven. Pierce the onion halves with the cloves; add to the pan along with the remaining 1 teaspoon salt. Add 1 quart of water; bring just to a boil over medium-high heat. Add the chicken and sausages plus additional water if necessary to cover. Return to a simmer; reduce the heat to medium-low. Poach until the chicken is no longer pink in the thickest portion when cut with a knife, 12 to 15 minutes. Remove the chicken, sausages, and vegetables with a slotted spoon; discard the onion. (Reserve the broth for another use.) Let the chicken, sausages, and vegetables rest briefly until cool enough to handle, about 10 minutes. Cut the chicken into thin slices; slice the sausages on the diagonal. Slice the vegetables into matchsticks (julienne).

Toss the mesclun mix with the vinaigrette in a medium bowl; divide among four plates. Fan out the chicken slices in the center of each plate. Arrange the sausage slices around the chicken. Scatter the julienned vegetables over the salads; top with the vrilles de vignes or the grape leaves. Sprinkle with peppercorns and serve immediately.

✳

TRUCS:

CHIFFONADE IS A TERM USED TO DESCRIBE THINLY SLICED STRIPS OF A GREEN, LEAFY INGREDIENT, OFTEN LETTUCE, SORREL, OR BASIL. TO CUT SOMETHING IN CHIFFONADE, ROLL A STACK OF LEAVES TIGHTLY, CIGAR FASHION, THEN CUT ACROSS THE ROLL TO FORM THIN RIBBONS OF GREEN.

USE THE REST OF THE JARRED OR CANNED BRINED GRAPE LEAVES FOR STUFFING WITH RICE AND MEAT MIXTURES AS THE GREEKS WOULD DO FOR DOLMADES.

Vietnamese Chicken
and Rice Noodle Salad

Before America fought and lost in Vietnam, the French had their turn and because of these ties, many Vietnamese emigrated to France. Walking down narrow roads in small French towns, it is not uncommon to find a Vietnamese restaurant. I discovered this salad in one little six-table outpost of Indochine cooking many years ago while touring the French countryside. Now I can sample Vietnamese cuisine both in France and at home in Minnesota, for America's war efforts led to a similar migration to our state.

MAKES 4 SERVINGS

⅓ cup sugar

5 tablespoons rice vinegar

2 tablespoons nuoc mâm (fish sauce)

½ teaspoon Vietnamese or Chinese
   chili-garlic sauce

One-half 7-ounce package Thai thin rice noodles,
   vermicelli-style

1 cup carrots sliced into 2-inch-long
   matchsticks (julienne)

4 cups torn romaine lettuce

1 cup fresh bean sprouts

¼ cup fresh cilantro leaves plus 4 sprigs
   for garnish

¼ cup torn fresh mint

¼ cup torn fresh basil

3 cups sliced cooked chicken

1 cup cucumbers sliced into 2-inch-long
   matchsticks (julienne)

½ cup chopped green onions

½ cup chopped peanuts

To make the sauce, combine the sugar and ⅓ cup of water in a small saucepan; heat over medium heat, stirring constantly, until boiling and the sugar is dissolved, 3 to 4 minutes. Remove from the heat; stir in 3 tablespoons of the rice vinegar. Pour into a bowl; stir in the nuoc mâm and chili-garlic sauce. Let the sauce cool.

Heat 4 cups of water in a medium saucepan over high heat until boiling. Remove from the heat; add the rice noodles. Let the noodles soak until soft and pliable, about 10 minutes, stirring occasionally. Drain.

Meanwhile, toss the carrots with the remaining 2 tablespoons of rice vinegar; let marinate while the noodles soak.

Mix the lettuce, bean sprouts, the ¼ cup of cilantro leaves, the mint, and basil together. Divide the lettuce mixture evenly among four shallow bowls. Add the noodles to the bowls, placing on one side. Add the chicken, placing opposite the noodles. Add the cucumbers, arranging on one side of the chicken; add the carrots, arranging on the other side of the chicken. Scatter the green onions and peanuts over the tops; garnish each with a cilantro sprig. Serve the sauce in individual small bowls, allowing each person to spoon the desired amount of sauce over his or her salad.

TRUC:

THE BETTER THE INGREDIENTS, THE BETTER THE SAUCE WILL BE. LOOK FOR RICE VINEGAR OF ABOUT 4.5 PERCENT ACIDITY. IT SHOULD HAVE A MILD, DELICATE TANG. TRY TO BUY AUTHENTIC, IMPORTED FISH SAUCE IF AT ALL POSSIBLE; THE MORE GENERIC VARIETY AVAILABLE IN MOST SUPERMARKETS JUST DOESN'T HAVE THE SAME FLAVOR BUT WILL DO IF IT'S THE ONLY THING AVAILABLE. I LIKE THE THREE CRABS BRAND THAT I BUY AT A LOCAL ASIAN STORE, WELL STOCKED WITH VIETNAMESE INGREDIENTS.

CHICKEN AND GARLIC SOUP

Simultaneously elegant and earthy, with an egg yolk–enriched broth substantially laced with garlic, this soup is guaranteed to be good for what might ail you.

MAKES 4 SERVINGS

5 cups Bouillon de Poule (page 14) or 5 cups
   reduced-sodium chicken broth
6 large whole garlic cloves, peeled and crushed
One 6- to 8-ounce boneless, skinless
   chicken breast
6 fresh sage leaves
¾ cup shredded carrot, optional
2 large egg yolks

Bring the bouillon and garlic cloves just to a boil over medium heat in a Dutch oven. Add the chicken; reduce the heat to medium-low. Poach until the chicken is no longer pink in the thickest portion when cut with a knife, 12 to 15 minutes. Remove the pot from the heat and remove the chicken breast. Add the sage leaves to the pot; cover and let steep for 10 minutes.

Remove and discard the sage leaves. Remove the garlic cloves and finely mince. Return to the pot. Add the shredded carrot, if using; return the pot to medium heat and simmer for 5 minutes.

Meanwhile, when cool enough to handle, slice the chicken breast into thin strips.

Whisk the yolks in the bottom of a soup tureen or large bowl. Stir in the simmering broth; add the chicken and serve.

TRUC:

Cooking garlic rounds out and mellows its more assertive qualities. Beware of recipes calling for large quantities of raw garlic; the harsh taste is often overwhelming. Instead, poach the garlic briefly before using it, as in this recipe.

COUNTRY-STYLE CHICKEN TERRINE

Every little restaurant seems to have a terrine maison—*a house terrine*—*or offers one from the charcuterie down the street. Sometimes made with chicken, sometimes rabbit or duck, it seems no matter what the building blocks, this form of rustic pâté makes an outstanding first course or appetizer. Named for the rectangular or oval container used in baking, terrines can be sliced straight from the mold or removed and served on a decorative platter.*

MAKES 24 APPETIZER SERVINGS OR 8 FIRST COURSE SERVINGS

8 ounces inexpensive, thin-sliced bacon

½ cup coarsely chopped pitted Nyons or kalamata olives

3 tablespoons Cognac

1 pound mild bulk pork sausage

2 large eggs

3 cups diced cooked chicken

½ cup pine nuts

3 tablespoons chopped shallots

2 teaspoons herbes de Provence

¾ teaspoon salt

½ teaspoon freshly ground pepper

½ cup diced roasted red bell pepper (from jar)

Preheat the oven to 350°F. Line the bottom and sides of a 1½-quart terrine or casserole with strips of bacon. Soak the olives in the Cognac for 10 minutes in a small bowl.

Mix the pork sausage and eggs together in a medium bowl. Add the olive-Cognac mixture, chicken, pine nuts, shallots, herbes de Provence, salt, and pepper; mix gently to combine. Gently stir in the roasted red bell pepper. Spoon into the prepared mold; top with strips of bacon. Place the mold in a shallow baking pan. Place in the oven; add hot water to the shallow pan to a depth of about 1 inch. Bake, covered tightly with aluminum foil and a lid, if available, for about 1½ hours or until a thermometer inserted in the center of the terrine registers 180°F. Remove the lid, if using; lay several cans on the foil to compress the pâté. Refrigerate overnight.

✳

TRUC:

INEXPENSIVE, THIN-SLICED BACON MAKES THE PERFECT CASING FOR THIS TERRINE. WITHOUT A GREAT DEAL OF FLAVOR AND SUBSTANCE, IT CONTRIBUTES JUST THE RIGHT AMOUNT OF EXTERIOR FAT NEEDED AS THE TERRINE BAKES AND SUBSTITUTES NICELY FOR THE *LARD GRAS* THE FRENCH WOULD USE.

VELOUTÉ DE POULET

CREAM OF CHICKEN SOUP

Velouté is a French cooking term most commonly applied to a stock-based white sauce. When used to describe a soup, you can predict it will contain the qualities its name implies—a velvet texture and voluptuous creaminess.

MAKES 6 SERVINGS

5 cups Bouillon de Poule (page 14) or reduced-
   sodium chicken broth
One 6- to 8-ounce boneless, skinless chicken
   breast
½ cup carrots cut into 1-inch-long
   matchsticks (julienne)
4 tablespoons (½ stick) salted butter
½ cup all-purpose flour
¾ cup heavy cream
2 large egg yolks
Fresh tarragon leaves for garnish

Bring the bouillon to a boil over medium-high heat in a medium saucepan. Add the chicken and carrots; reduce the heat to medium-low and poach until the chicken is no longer pink in the thickest portion when cut with a knife, 12 to 15 minutes. Strain, reserving the bouillon. Let the chicken cool slightly. When cool enough to handle, cut the chicken into small dice.

Melt the butter over medium heat in a large saucepan; stir in the flour to form a paste (roux). Cook, stirring frequently to remove the floury taste, 1 to 2 minutes. Whisk in the warm bouillon until smooth. Continue to cook, whisking frequently, until the mixture comes to a boil. Boil to thicken slightly, 3 to 4 minutes. Whisk in ½ cup of the cream; remove the saucepan from the heat.

Whisk together the remaining ¼ cup of cream and the egg yolks, then whisk into the bouillon mixture (velouté). Return to the heat; cook, whisking constantly over medium-low heat, until heated through and thickened slightly, 1 to 2 minutes. Do not boil. Add the diced chicken and the carrots. Garnish with a few leaves of tarragon and serve.

TRUC:

FOR A QUICK WAY TO CUT RAW VEGETABLES INTO JULIENNE, USE THE CUTTING BLADE DESIGNED FOR JUST THAT PURPOSE ON THE FRENCH SLICING DEVICE CALLED A MANDO-LINE. OR THINLY SLICE THE VEGETABLES, STACK THE SLICES, AND THEN CUT THE SLICES INTO MATCHSTICKS.

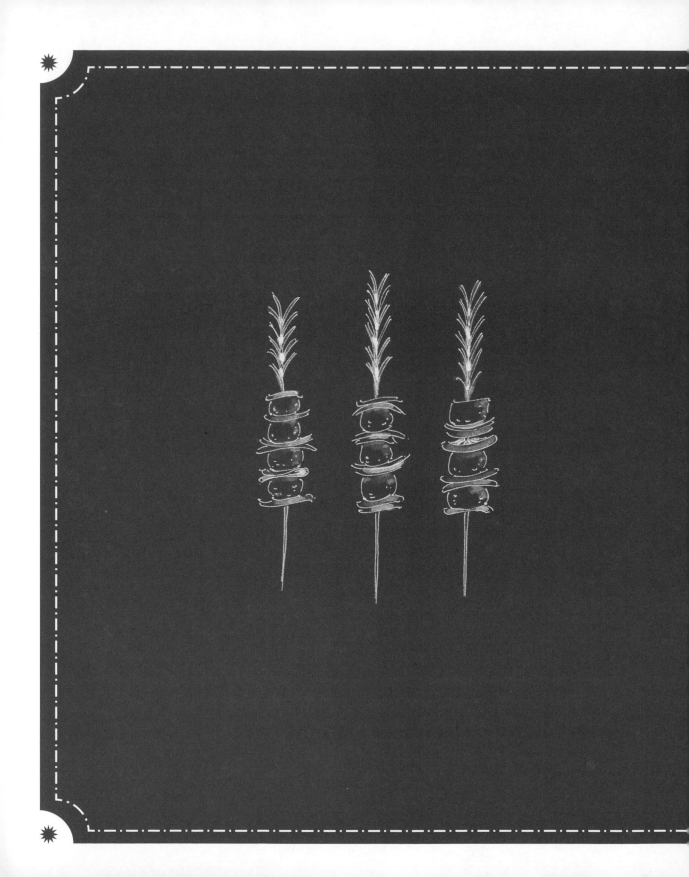

POULETS VITES

Sautéed, Simmered, and Grilled Main Courses

BONELESS CHICKEN BREAST SAUTÉ WITH ARTICHOKES

*I*n Provence, beautiful, violet-tinged artichokes beckon fetchingly from market stalls and combine with garlic and lemon in this appealing, rustic sauté. Our baby green artichokes work just as well, or, if you're pressed for time, a package of frozen hearts can make this recipe even speedier.

Because potatoes pair so well with artichokes, they make the ideal accompaniment to this dish. Simply roast, boil, or steam small red potatoes in their skins and toss them with a bit of extra virgin olive oil, salt, and pepper before serving.

MAKES 4 SERVINGS

3 tablespoons fresh lemon juice

12 baby artichokes or one 9-ounce package frozen artichoke hearts, thawed

3 tablespoons olive oil

1 small onion, diced

2 teaspoons minced garlic

¾ cup reduced-sodium chicken broth

Four 6- to 8-ounce boneless, skinless chicken breasts

⅛ teaspoon salt

⅛ teaspoon freshly ground pepper

¼ teaspoon dried thyme

Fill a medium bowl half full of water; add 2 tablespoons of the lemon juice. Trim each baby artichoke by removing its stem and peeling off the exterior leaves until the core is pale yellow except for the top third. Cut off the top third and halve the artichoke. As the artichokes are trimmed, place in the lemon water.

Heat 2 tablespoons of the olive oil in a large
skillet over medium-high heat. When hot, add
the onion. Drain the artichokes well; add to the
skillet. Sauté until browned, 4 to 5 minutes.
Stir in the garlic; sauté until fragrant, 30
seconds to 1 minute. Add the broth; cover
and reduce the heat to medium-low. Simmer
for 5 minutes. Pour into a medium bowl. Add
the remaining 1 tablespoon of olive oil to the
skillet; when hot, add the breasts, seasoned
with the salt and pepper. Sauté until golden
brown on both sides, 2 to 3 minutes per side.
Return the artichoke-broth mixture to the
skillet; sprinkle with the thyme. Reduce the
heat to low and cook, covered, turning once,
until the chicken is no longer pink in the
thickest portion when cut with a knife, 4 to 5
minutes per side. Remove the chicken to a
platter and cover with foil to keep warm.
Increase the heat to high; add the remaining
1 tablespoon of lemon juice and boil the
artichoke-broth mixture until reduced slightly,
3 to 4 minutes. Pour over the chicken and
serve immediately.

✳

TRUC:

SINCE ARTICHOKES DISCOLOR EASILY, IT'S
IMPORTANT TO KEEP THEM IN ACIDULATED
WATER AFTER TRIMMING. LEMON JUICE
PROVIDES THE NECESSARY ACID WHILE
ENHANCING THE ARTICHOKE'S FLAVOR.

BASQUE-STYLE BONELESS
CHICKEN BREASTS

---

*T*he Basque region runs through the heart of the Pyrénées, the mountain chain separating France and Spain. Its savage beauty seems to have influenced its people. To this day, separatists from the area are fiercely protective of their unique culture. As a college student, I stayed in Saint-Jean-Pied-de-Port on the French-Spanish border, only to discover later, while reading Hemingway's The Sun Also Rises, that he too loved its rugged wildness. The following dish is a bistro and café favorite throughout France but its spicy roots start here. I've streamlined the dish by using boneless, skinless chicken breasts instead of whole, cut-up chickens. Serve it with cooked rice for a complete main course.

MAKES 4 SERVINGS

2 tablespoons olive oil

1 large onion, cut into ½-inch dice

1 red bell pepper, cut into ½-inch dice

1 green bell pepper, cut into ½-inch dice

1 teaspoon dried ground piment d'Espelette or
  2 jalapeño chiles, seeded and chopped, plus
  ⅛ teaspoon cayenne

4 ounces jambon de Bayonne or Serrano ham,
  finely diced

1 tablespoon minced garlic

2 medium tomatoes, coarsely chopped
  (about ¾ pound)

½ cup white wine

Four 6- to 8-ounce boneless, skinless
  chicken breasts

¼ teaspoon salt

⅛ teaspoon freshly ground pepper

Heat 1 tablespoon of the olive oil in a large skillet over medium-high heat. When hot, add the onion, bell peppers, and piment d'Espelette; cook until beginning to soften, 4 to 5 minutes. Stir in the jambon de Bayonne and garlic; cook until fragrant, 30 seconds to 1 minute. Add the tomatoes and white wine; cook for an additional 5 minutes. Remove to a bowl.

Add the remaining 1 tablespoon of olive oil to the same skillet. Add the breasts, seasoned with the salt and pepper; sauté until well browned on both sides, 3 to 4 minutes per side. Return the onion-pepper mixture to the skillet; reduce the heat to low. Cover; cook, turning once, until the chicken is no longer pink in the thickest portion when cut with a knife, 3 to 4 minutes per side. Serve.

✳

TRUC:

PIMENT D'ESPELETTE IS A SMALL, MODERATELY SPICY PEPPER GROWN IN THE BASQUE REGION. WHEN TRAVELING, KEEP YOUR EYES OPEN IN MARKETS AND GROCERY STORES FOR SMALL CONTAINERS OF UNUSUAL SEASONINGS TO BRING HOME AS SOUVENIRS. LIKE PROUST AND HIS MADELEINES, YOU WILL FIND THEIR AROMAS WILL SUMMON VIVID MEMORIES. THEY ALSO MAKE MUCH APPRECIATED GIFTS.

BLANCS DE VOLAILLE BONNE FEMME

Rustic Boneless Chicken Breast Sauté

Bonne femme *translates as good woman or good wife and the term, in cooking, usually connotes a rustic, country style of cooking, often with slab bacon, onions, and potatoes.* Poulet bonne femme, *the more customary treatment for chicken, uses bone-in chicken pieces and cooks a bit more slowly. I've taken the liberty of speeding up the process using boneless, skinless breasts. Today, the good wife or good husband—the* bon mari—*gets dinner to the table as quickly as possible.*

MAKES 4 SERVINGS

2 tablespoons canola oil

½ cup diced thick-cut mild bacon

Four 6- to 8-ounce boneless, skinless
   chicken breasts

¼ teaspoon salt

¼ teaspoon freshly ground pepper

¾ cup frozen whole baby onions, thawed

2 cups diced cooked boiling potatoes
   (about ¾-inch dice)

Heat the canola oil in a large skillet over medium-high heat. When hot, add the diced bacon; sauté until crisp, 4 to 5 minutes. Remove with a slotted spoon; drain on paper towels. Add the breasts, seasoned with ⅛ teaspoon of the salt and ⅛ teaspoon of the pepper, along with the onions. Sauté until golden brown on both sides, 2 to 3 minutes per side. Reduce the heat to low, cover, and cook, turning once, until the chicken is no longer pink in the thickest portion when cut with a knife, 4 to 5 minutes per side. Remove the breasts to a warm platter; top with the onions. Cover with aluminum foil to keep warm.

BISTRO CHICKEN **60**

Increase the heat to medium-high. When the pan is hot, add the potatoes and cook for 4 to 5 minutes or until browned; season with the remaining ⅛ teaspoon of salt and ⅛ teaspoon of pepper. Stir in the bacon. Scatter the potato mixture over the breasts and serve immediately.

✳

TRUCS:

SINCE OUR SALT PORK TENDS TO BE A BIT TOUGH WHEN SIMPLY SAUTÉED AND NOT SIMMERED, BACON IS A BETTER CHOICE HERE. IF TIME ALLOWS, AND FOR A MORE AUTHENTIC TASTE, DROP THE BACON IN SIMMERING WATER FOR ABOUT 5 MINUTES AND PAT THE DICED PIECES DRY BEFORE SAUTÉING. IT REMOVES SOME OF THE SMOKY FLAVOR.

FOR COOKED POTATOES IN A HURRY, QUARTER 2 OR 3 MEDIUM BOILING POTATOES AND COOK THEM IN A MICROWAVE-SAFE COVERED CONTAINER WITH A TABLESPOON OF WATER ON HIGH IN YOUR MICROWAVE UNTIL BARELY TENDER, ABOUT 8 MINUTES. IF YOU START THEM BEFORE SAUTÉING THE BACON, THEY'LL BE SLIGHTLY COOLED AND READY FOR DICING WHILE THE CHICKEN FINISHES COOKING. SYNCHRONIZING YOUR TIMING IS ONE OF THE WAYS TO GET A MEAL DONE QUICKLY.

BONELESS CHICKEN BREASTS STUFFED WITH CAMEMBERT

I love going to buy Camembert from my favorite cheese shop in Paris—Cantin, located in the seventh arrondissement. The staff will select just the right fragrant, white wheel of cheese based on whether you want one for that day, tomorrow, or the day after. As an added bonus, the resident Labrador might be there to greet you as well.

MAKES 4 SERVINGS

One-half 250-gram wheel Camembert cheese
Four 6- to 8-ounce boneless, skinless
   chicken breasts
¼ teaspoon salt
⅛ teaspoon freshly ground pepper
2 tablespoons salted butter
2 tablespoons canola oil
8 ounces sliced white button mushrooms
⅓ cup reduced-sodium chicken broth

Trim the rind from the Camembert; cut the Camembert into 4 pieces. Press the tenderloin flap outward on each breast, leaving it attached. Cut a 3-inch-wide pocket halfway through the thickness of each breast, centering the cut and cutting horizontally toward the thicker side. Cut until the pocket reaches to about ½ inch from the thicker side. Insert 1 piece of Camembert into each pocket, cutting and trimming as necessary to form a thin strip of Camembert in each pocket. Tuck the top edge of each pocket inward and fold the tenderloin edge over the pocket like the flap of an envelope. Tuck the bottom point of the breast upward. Seal the edges securely with toothpicks; season with the salt and pepper.

Heat the butter and 1 tablespoon of the canola oil in a large skillet over medium-high heat. When sizzling, add the mushrooms; cook until tender, 4 to 6 minutes. Remove to a bowl. Add the remaining 1 tablespoon of canola oil; add the breasts, sealed side down. Sauté until golden brown on both sides, 2 to 3 minutes per side. Reduce the heat to low; add the broth. Sprinkle the mushrooms over the breasts; cover and cook until the chicken is no longer pink when carefully cut at the thickest portion of the unstuffed top of the breast, 8 to 10 minutes. Remove the chicken to a serving platter.

Increase the heat to high and reduce the cooking juices slightly, 1 to 2 minutes. Spoon the mushrooms and juices over the breasts and serve.

✳

TRUC:

HERE IN AMERICA, WHEN SELECTING A CAMEMBERT, PRESS THE CHEESE GENTLY; IT SHOULD YIELD SLIGHTLY. CHECK THE AROMA IF POSSIBLE; IT SHOULD HAVE A MUSHROOM-LIKE SMELL WITHOUT ANY HINTS OF AMMONIA.

BONELESS CHICKEN BREAST SAUTÉ WITH MUSHROOMS

*C*hampignons de Paris (Parisian mushrooms) are the small, white button mushrooms we know so well from the supermarket produce section. The French learned that mushrooms could be cultivated and discovered that the old quarries or "caves" around Paris provided an excellent growing medium. Although urban sprawl has displaced production, the name remains.

MAKES 4 SERVINGS

2 tablespoons canola oil

2 tablespoons salted butter

8 ounces white button mushrooms, quartered

¼ cup minced shallots

Four 6- to 8-ounce boneless, skinless
   chicken breasts

¼ teaspoon salt

⅛ teaspoon freshly ground pepper

½ cup reduced-sodium chicken broth

½ cup white wine

½ cup crème fraîche

1 tablespoon chopped fresh chives

1 tablespoon chopped fresh chervil

1 tablespoon chopped fresh tarragon

1 tablespoon chopped fresh parsley

Heat the canola oil and butter in a large skillet over medium heat. When sizzling, add the mushrooms and shallots. Sauté until just beginning to soften, 2 to 3 minutes. Push to the edges of the skillet; add the breasts, seasoned with the salt and pepper. Sauté until golden brown on both sides, 3 to 4 minutes per side. Reduce the heat to low; add the broth and white wine. Cover; cook, turning once, until the chicken is no longer pink in the thickest portion when cut with a knife, 4 to 5 minutes per side. Remove the breasts; arrange on a serving platter; cover with aluminum foil to keep warm. Whisk the crème fraîche into the skillet; increase the heat to high and cook to reduce and thicken slightly, 2 to 3 minutes.

Meanwhile, finely chop the chives, chervil, tarragon, and parsley together. Pour the reduced sauce over the breasts; sprinkle with the chopped herbs and serve.

✳

TRUC:
DESPITE COOKING MYTHS TO THE CONTRARY, YOU CAN WASH MUSHROOMS INSTEAD OF GOING THROUGH THE PAINFULLY SLOW PROCESS OF BRUSHING THEM TO REMOVE EXCESS GRIT. DON'T SOAK THE MUSHROOMS BUT CLEAN THEM QUICKLY WITH WATER JUST BEFORE USING, DRAIN WELL, AND PAT DRY WITH PAPER TOWELS.

BONELESS CHICKEN BREASTS STUFFED WITH GOAT CHEESE AND BASIL

Goat cheese and basil are one of the soul-mate combinations of the food world. Stuffed into chicken breasts, the creamy cheese bastes the white meat from the inside and the sunny taste of basil shines through every bite.

MAKES 4 SERVINGS

Four 6- to 8-ounce boneless, skinless
  chicken breasts

¼ cup chopped fresh basil

One 3½- to 4-ounce log of chèvre, such as
  Montrachet, cut into 4 sticks

⅛ teaspoon salt

⅛ teaspoon freshly ground pepper

1 tablespoon olive oil

1 tablespoon salted butter plus 2 tablespoons
  cold salted butter, cut into bits

⅓ cup reduced-sodium chicken broth

½ cup white wine

Press the tenderloin flap outward on each breast, leaving it attached. Cut a 3-inch-wide pocket halfway through the thickness of each breast, centering the cut and cutting horizontally toward the thicker side. Cut until the pocket reaches to about ½ inch from the thicker side. Insert 1 tablespoon of the basil into each pocket, then 1 stick of chèvre. Tuck the top edge of each pocket inward and fold the tenderloin edge over the pocket like the flap of an envelope. Tuck the bottom point of the breast upward. Seal the edges securely with toothpicks; season with the salt and pepper.

Heat the olive oil and the 1 tablespoon of butter in a large skillet over medium-high heat. When sizzling, add the stuffed breasts, sealed side down. Sauté until golden brown on both sides, 2 to 3 minutes per side. Reduce the heat to low; add the broth. Cover; cook until the chicken is no longer pink when carefully cut at the thickest portion of the unstuffed top of the breast, 8 to 10 minutes. Remove the chicken to a platter; cover with aluminum foil to keep warm.

Increase the heat to high and add the white wine. Boil until reduced by half, 4 to 5 minutes. Remove from the heat; whisk in the 2 tablespoons of cold butter until incorporated. Pour the sauce over the chicken; serve immediately.

TRUC:

WHISKING COLD BUTTER INTO A WINE REDUCTION IS A USEFUL TECHNIQUE FOR THICKENING AND ENRICHING THE SAUCE AT THE SAME TIME. MAKE SURE THE BUTTER IS WELL CHILLED; OTHERWISE IT SIMPLY MELTS AND SEPARATES INSTEAD OF EMULSIFYING WITH THE WINE.

BLANCS DE VOLAILLE AUX CREVETTES

BONELESS CHICKEN BREAST SAUTÉ WITH SHRIMP

Normandy is blessed with both farms and an ocean as a source for ingredients, making this delicate combination of poultry, seafood, and fresh dairy cream a showcase for the best of the region.

MAKES 4 SERVINGS

½ pound medium shrimp

2 tablespoons salted butter

Four 5-ounce boneless, skinless chicken breasts

¼ teaspoon salt

⅛ teaspoon freshly ground pepper

½ cup white wine

½ cup heavy cream

1 teaspoon fresh lemon juice

2 teaspoons chopped fresh tarragon or

 ¾ teaspoon dried

Shell and devein the shrimp; reserve the shells. Heat the butter in a large skillet over medium heat. When sizzling, add the shrimp shells; sauté for 2 to 3 minutes, stirring occasionally. Remove the shells to a small bowl. Season the breasts with the salt and pepper and add to the skillet; sauté until golden brown on both sides, 3 to 4 minutes per side. Reduce the heat to low; add the white wine. Return the shrimp shells to the skillet. Cover; cook for 4 minutes. Turn the breasts; add the shrimp. Cover; cook until the breasts are no longer pink in the thickest portion when cut with a knife, 3 to 4 minutes. Remove the chicken and shrimp to a platter; cover with aluminum foil to keep warm.

Strain the cooking liquid to remove the shells; return to the skillet. Increase the heat to high; add the cream, lemon juice, and tarragon. Cook until lightly thickened, 3 to 5 minutes. Pour the sauce over the chicken and shrimp. Serve.

✳

TRUC:

ADDING THE SHELLS TO THE SIMMERING COOKING LIQUID TRANSFERS THEIR BRINY TASTE INTO THE SAUCE. IT'S A GOOD IDEA TO SAVE SHRIMP AND LOBSTER SHELLS IN THE FREEZER TO USE LATER WHEN MAKING SEAFOOD STOCKS AND SOUPS.

BONELESS CHICKEN BREASTS
STUFFED WITH FOIE GRAS

Foie gras may seem an unlikely ingredient in a bistro cookbook but it's not. Certainly not every bistro serves it but enough do that I'm not startled to find foie gras in salads or offered as a first course choice. What did surprise me one rainy April day in Nice was to find it used as stuffing. Having flown into Nice instead of Paris as I usually do, I set out to find my ritual roast chicken. Since it was so wet outside, I stumbled into the first little restaurant I found. They didn't have roast chicken, an almost unheard-of occurrence, but they had the following instead. It served the purpose nicely.

MAKES 6 SERVINGS

One 3-ounce portion canned foie gras of duck
  or goose
Six 6- to 8-ounce boneless, skinless chicken
  breasts, tenderloin section removed
¼ teaspoon salt
⅛ teaspoon freshly ground pepper
1 tablespoon salted butter
1 tablespoon Cognac or brandy
¼ cup all-purpose flour
One 14-ounce can reduced-sodium chicken broth

Trim the fat from the block of foie gras; reserve. Cut the foie gras into 6 sticks about ½ inch wide and about 2 inches long. Carefully butterfly the breasts; begin at one side of each breast and slice the flesh into two thinner pieces, stopping before cutting through the other side. Open the two pieces, flattening the attached portion in the center to form a large, thin piece of chicken. Place a foie gras stick in the center of each breast. Fold the flesh to form a package around the foie gras; fasten carefully with toothpicks. Season with the salt and pepper.

Heat the butter in a large skillet over medium heat. When sizzling, add the breasts; sauté until golden brown on both sides, 3 to 4 minutes per side. Reduce the heat to low; cover and cook, turning once, until the chicken is no longer pink when carefully cut at the thickest portion of the unstuffed top of the breast, 4 to 5 minutes per side. Remove the breasts to a platter. Cover with aluminum foil to keep warm.

Add the Cognac to the skillet; increase the heat to medium. Scrape up any brown bits; cook briefly to evaporate the Cognac, 1 to 2 minutes. Add 2 tablespoons of the reserved fat from the foie gras. (Supplement with butter if necessary to make 2 tablespoons.) When melted, whisk in the flour; cook briefly to remove any floury taste, 1 to 2 minutes. Whisk in the broth; bring to a boil. Boil to thicken slightly, 1 to 2 minutes. Pour the sauce over the breasts and serve.

TRUC:

BUY EITHER DUCK OR GOOSE FOIE GRAS IN A SMALL CAN AND SAVE PART OF IT TO SERVE CHILLED AS AN APPETIZER. THE REMAINDER CAN GO IN THIS DECADENT MAIN COURSE. I BUY A SMALL CAN OF FOIE GRAS TO BRING HOME EVERY TIME I GO TO FRANCE BUT IT'S A SPLURGE EVEN THERE; FOR A CHEAPER VERSION, USE DUCK LIVER PÂTÉ

BONELESS CHICKEN BREASTS NIÇOISE

An absolute must when visiting Nice is a visit to the spectacular food market in the old section of the city. Along with seasonal produce, vendors set up incredible displays of olives. Among them are the briny, black niçoise olives featured in this recipe. You can find them in specialty food markets here in this country or you can substitute Greek kalamata olives, if necessary.

For dark meat lovers, this dish adapts very well to skinless, boneless thighs. Use about 12 thighs; sauté them in batches and return them to the skillet after reducing the tomato mixture. Thigh meat takes a bit longer to cook, so increase the final cooking time to 5 to 8 minutes per side.

MAKES 6 SERVINGS

2 tablespoons olive oil

Six 6- to 8-ounce boneless, skinless
   chicken breasts

1 large onion, chopped

1 tablespoon minced garlic

One 15-ounce can diced tomatoes, undrained

1 cup pitted and coarsely chopped niçoise or
   kalamata olives

½ cup red wine

½ cup reduced-sodium chicken broth

1 tablespoon Pernod, optional

1 teaspoon herbes de Provence

Heat the olive oil in a large skillet over medium-high heat. When hot, add the breasts; sauté until well browned on both sides, 3 to 4 minutes per side. Remove and set aside. Add the onion and sauté until softened, 3 to 4 minutes; add the garlic and continue to cook until fragrant, 30 seconds to 1 minute. Add the tomatoes with their juice and crush lightly with a fork. Add the olives, red wine, broth, Pernod, if using, and herbes de Provence. Cook until reduced and thickened slightly, 8 to 10 minutes. Return the breasts to the skillet; reduce the heat to low. Cook, covered, turning once, until the chicken is no longer pink in the thickest portion when cut with a knife, 3 to 4 minutes per side. Serve.

To prepare ahead, refrigerate, covered, until just before serving. Reheat the chicken slowly over low heat in the tomato-olive mixture until just heated through. Do not overcook.

TRUC:

USE CANNED, DICED TOMATOES INSTEAD OF FRESH WHEN TOMATOES ARE OUT OF SEASON. THE FLAVOR IS FAR SUPERIOR TO THAT OF THE PALLID, ROUND, CARDBOARD-TEXTURED IMPOSTORS FOUND IN MOST SUPERMARKET PRODUCE DEPARTMENTS.

BONELESS CHICKEN BREAST SAUTÉ WITH WALNUT SAUCE

In southwestern France, the sauce for this dish is called sauce aillade *(garlic sauce) and is equally agreeable served with sautéed duck breasts—magrets de canard.*

MAKES 4 SERVINGS

1 medium garlic clove

¾ cup walnut pieces

½ teaspoon salt

⅛ teaspoon freshly ground pepper plus a pinch

1 tablespoon fresh lemon juice

6 tablespoons imported walnut oil

Four 6- to 8-ounce boneless, skinless
   chicken breasts

1 tablespoon peanut or canola oil

1 tablespoon salted butter

1 tablespoon chopped fresh parsley

1 tablespoon chopped fresh tarragon

With the motor running, drop the garlic into the bowl of a food processor fitted with a metal blade. Scrape down the sides; add ½ cup of the walnut pieces, ¼ teaspoon of the salt, and the pinch of pepper. Process until finely ground, scraping down the sides once or twice. Add 2 tablespoons of water and the lemon juice; pulse to blend, scraping down the sides and bottom as necessary. Slowly add the walnut oil to form a creamy sauce aillade. Set aside until ready to serve.

Season the breasts with the remaining ¼
teaspoon of salt and ⅛ teaspoon of pepper.
Sauté the remaining ¼ cup of walnut pieces in a
large skillet over medium heat until just beginning to color, 5 to 8 minutes; remove to a bowl.
Heat the peanut oil and butter in the skillet;
when sizzling, add the breasts and sauté until
well browned on both sides, 4 to 5 minutes per
side. Reduce the heat to low; cover and cook,
turning once, until the chicken is no longer
pink in the thickest portion when cut with a
knife, 3 to 4 minutes per side. Sprinkle with
the parsley and tarragon; garnish with the walnut pieces. Serve the sauce aillade on the side.

✳

TRUC:

MAKE SURE TO USE THE WONDERFUL
IMPORTED WALNUT OIL AVAILABLE IN
SPECIALTY STORES FOR THIS RECIPE. THE
DOMESTIC VERSIONS DON'T HAVE THE
ESSENTIAL TOASTED QUALITY NECESSARY TO
DELIVER A TRUE WALNUT BASE TO THE SAUCE.

BONELESS CHICKEN BREAST SAUTÉ WITH THYME

*T*hese chicken breasts emerge from the skillet flecked with deeply browned shallots and bits of thyme. Serve them over galettes de pommes de terre—*crisp disks of shredded potato pancakes.*

MAKES 4 SERVINGS

GALETTES DE POMMES DE TERRE

¾ *pound Idaho russet potatoes*

2 tablespoons peanut oil

⅛ *teaspoon salt*

⅛ *teaspoon freshly ground pepper*

BLANCS DE VOLAILLE AU THYM

1 tablespoon salted butter

¼ *cup chopped shallots*

Four 6- to 8-ounce boneless, skinless chicken breasts

2 teaspoons chopped fresh thyme leaves or ¾ *teaspoon crumbled dried thyme*

½ *teaspoon salt*

⅛ *teaspoon freshly ground pepper*

½ *cup white wine*

Preheat the oven to 250°F. For the galettes, peel the potatoes and shred them in a food processor just before cooking.

Heat the peanut oil in a large nonstick skillet over medium-high heat. When hot, press one-fourth of the shredded potatoes into a 3- to 4-inch disk; place in the skillet. (Don't worry if the potatoes don't stick together well. They will adhere to each other as they cook.) Repeat with the remaining potatoes. Cook until medium brown and crisp on both sides, 3 to 4 minutes per side. Remove to a baking sheet; hold in the oven while preparing the chicken. (Season with the salt and pepper just before serving.)

TRUC:

USE IDAHO RUSSETS WHEN FRYING. THEIR HIGH STARCH CONTENT GIVES THEM A PROPERLY CRUNCHY EXTERIOR AND A SOFT, FLUFFY INNER TEXTURE. PEANUT OIL GIVES A THOROUGHLY FRENCH TASTE (ALTHOUGH ANY OIL WITH A RELATIVELY HIGH SMOKE POINT CAN BE USED); PEANUT OIL IS THE SAME OIL TRADITIONALLY USED TO PREPARE *POMMES FRITES* (FRENCH FRIES).

For the chicken, heat the butter in the same skillet over medium heat. Add the shallots; sauté until beginning to soften, 2 to 3 minutes. Season both sides of the breasts with the thyme, salt, and pepper. Add to the skillet; sauté until golden brown on both sides, 3 to 4 minutes per side. Add the white wine; reduce the heat to low and cook, turning once, until the chicken is no longer pink in the thickest portion when cut with a knife, 4 to 5 minutes per side. Remove to a platter.

Increase the heat to high and reduce the pan juices in the skillet slightly, 1 to 2 minutes.

To serve, season each galette with the salt and pepper and place 1 potato galette on each plate; top with a chicken breast. Drizzle the pan juices over all.

BLANCS DE VOLAILLE AU VERJUS
BONELESS CHICKEN BREAST SAUTÉ WITH VERJUS

Verjus is an old-fashioned condiment that is part of a trend in France to use ingredients "à l'ancienne." Made from the juice of wine grapes, it is left unfermented, resulting in a flavor somewhere between vinegar and wine. Tart and fresher tasting than vinegar, it sparks sauces more vividly than wine.

MAKES 4 SERVINGS

1 tablespoon canola oil

1 tablespoon salted butter plus 1 tablespoon cold salted butter

Four 6- to 8-ounce boneless, skinless chicken breasts

½ teaspoon salt

⅛ teaspoon freshly ground pepper

⅓ cup chopped shallots

⅔ cup verjus

¼ cup raisins

2 tablespoons chopped chives

Heat the canola oil and the 1 tablespoon of butter in a large skillet over medium-high heat. When sizzling, add the breasts, seasoned with the salt and pepper; sauté until well browned on one side, 3 to 4 minutes. Sprinkle with the shallots; turn and sauté until well browned on the other side, 3 to 4 minutes. Reduce the heat to low; add the verjus and raisins. Cover; cook, turning once, until the chicken is no longer pink in the thickest portion when cut with a knife, 3 to 4 minutes per side. Remove the chicken to a platter; cover with aluminum foil to keep warm.

Increase the heat to high and reduce the pan juices by half, scraping up any brown bits from the bottom of the pan, 4 to 5 minutes. Remove from the heat; whisk in the 1 tablespoon of cold butter. Pour the reduced verjus sauce over the breasts; garnish with the chopped chives and serve.

TRUC:

NO VERJUS? BUY TART GREEN GRAPES AND WHIRL ¾ CUP OF GRAPES WITH ½ CUP OF WATER IN A BLENDER. STRAIN AND USE THE LIQUID AS A SUBSTITUTE.

BROCHETTES DE VOLAILLE

CHICKEN KEBABS

Brochettes, or skewers, have a definite Mediterranean character. These plump portions of chicken, marinated with herbs and lemon, then grilled to perfection, will turn your own backyard into a seaside escape.

MAKES 4 SERVINGS

3 tablespoons fresh lemon juice plus 1 lemon,
   cut into 8 wedges

3 tablespoons olive oil

2 teaspoons minced garlic

2 teaspoons minced fresh thyme or
   ¾ teaspoon dried

2 teaspoons minced fresh oregano or
   ¾ teaspoon dried

½ teaspoon salt

¼ teaspoon freshly ground pepper

½ pound small new potatoes or red boiling
   potatoes, quartered

1¼ to 1½ pounds boneless, skinless chicken
   breasts, cut into 1½-inch cubes

1 small green bell pepper, cut into 1½-inch pieces

1 small red or yellow bell pepper, cut into
   1½-inch pieces

8 skewers

Combine the lemon juice, olive oil, garlic, thyme, oregano, salt, and pepper in a bowl; set aside.

Cook the potatoes in boiling salted water to cover in a saucepan until just tender, about 20 minutes; drain and let cool.

Meanwhile, combine the chicken with two-thirds of the marinade in a self-sealing bag. Let marinate, refrigerated, for 1 hour, turning once. When the potatoes are cool, combine with the bell peppers in a bowl; toss with the remaining one-third of the marinade.

Preheat the grill.

Thread the marinated chicken, potatoes, and peppers onto skewers; discard the marinade. Grill over medium-high heat, covered, on a gas grill or 4 to 6 inches from the coals on a charcoal grill, turning every 4 to 5 minutes, until the chicken is no longer pink in the thickest portion when cut with a knife, 16 to 20 minutes total. Place a lemon wedge on the end of each skewer; serve.

✳

TRUC:

SELF-SEALING PLASTIC BAGS ARE PERFECT FOR MARINATING. IT'S EASY ONCE EVERYTHING IS ADDED AND THE BAG IS SEALED TO GENTLY MASSAGE THE MARINADE OVER ALL THE CHICKEN PIECES. THEY TURN EASILY, ALLOWING THE POOLED MARINADE TO PENETRATE ALL SURFACES.

CHICKEN WITH CHERMOULA

Chermoula is another North African seasoning blend that has made its way into mainstream French cooking. Essentially a pre-grill marinade, it's most often used with fish but adapts well to the mild taste of chicken.

MAKES 4 SERVINGS

1½ teaspoons minced garlic
½ teaspoon salt
⅓ cup chopped fresh cilantro
⅓ cup chopped fresh parsley
1 teaspoon ground cumin
1 teaspoon paprika
½ teaspoon ground ginger
Pinch cayenne
2 tablespoons olive oil
1 tablespoon fresh lemon juice
Four 6- to 8-ounce boneless, skinless chicken breasts

To make the chermoula marinade, mash the garlic with the salt with the tines of a fork on a cutting board to form a paste. Sprinkle with the cilantro and parsley; finely chop until almost a paste. Transfer to a small bowl; stir in the cumin, paprika, ginger, and cayenne. Add the olive oil and lemon juice; stir.

Place the breasts in a shallow, rectangular glass dish. Spread half the chermoula over the surface of the chicken; turn the breasts and spread the remaining chermoula on the other side. Refrigerate, covered, and marinate for 1 hour.

Meanwhile, heat the grill.

Grill the chicken over medium heat, covered, on a gas grill or 4 to 6 inches from the coals on a charcoal grill, turning once, until the chicken is no longer pink in the thickest portion when cut with a knife, 5 to 8 minutes per side. Serve.

TRUC:

DID YOU KNOW THAT GRILLS AND BROILERS
PRODUCE THE SAME TYPE OF HEAT? FOOD IS
DIRECTLY EXPOSED TO THE HEAT SOURCE IN
BOTH CASES. SO, WHEN YOU DON'T WANT TO
FIRE UP THE GRILL, TURN TO YOUR STOVE'S
BROILER INSTEAD. OLD BROILING TIPS, SUCH
AS LEAVING THE OVEN DOOR AJAR WITH AN
ELECTRIC BROILER, OFTEN DON'T WORK WITH
NEW APPLIANCES, SO MAKE SURE YOU KNOW
YOUR MANUFACTURER'S RECOMMENDATIONS
BY CHECKING THE MANUAL.

CROUSTILLANTS DE BLANCS DE VOLAILLE

BONELESS CHICKEN BREASTS
IN PHYLLO

Past the fountain and down the road from our house in the village of Mollans is the Hôtel St. Marc. There the owners, Bernard and Christiane Deuwille, serve up what the French call un chaleureux accueil—a warm welcome—to their guests in both the hotel proper and their restaurant. On a warm July evening, while dining in their courtyard, I ordered this dish and was charmed.

MAKES 4 SERVINGS

8 tablespoons (1 stick) unsalted butter, softened

¾ teaspoon cinnamon

¼ teaspoon salt

⅛ teaspoon freshly ground pepper

1 tablespoon canola oil

Four 5-ounce boneless, skinless chicken breasts

1 Golden Delicious apple, peeled, cored, and diced

½ cup white wine

1 tablespoon Dijon mustard

Eight 17 × 12-inch leaves phyllo, thawed

½ cup heavy cream

Blend 7 tablespoons of the butter and ½ teaspoon of the cinnamon in a small saucepan; set aside. Line a baking sheet with parchment.

Combine the remaining ¼ teaspoon of cinnamon, the salt, and the pepper. Heat the canola oil and remaining 1 tablespoon of butter in a large skillet over medium heat. When sizzling, add the breasts, seasoned with the cinnamon-salt-pepper mixture; sauté until golden brown on both sides, 3 to 4 minutes per side. Reduce the heat to low; cover and cook, turning once, until the chicken is no longer pink in the thickest portion when cut with a knife, 4 to 5 minutes per side. Arrange the breasts in a single layer on a cookie sheet; place in the freezer to cool for about 15 minutes.

Meanwhile, put the apple in the skillet; increase the heat to medium-high and brown briefly, 2 to 3 minutes. Add the white wine and mustard; boil to reduce to about ⅓ cup, 2 to 3 minutes. Pour into a bowl; refrigerate, covered, until ready to complete the recipe.

Melt the cinnamon-butter mixture over low heat. Lay one sheet of phyllo lengthwise on the counter; brush lightly with the melted butter. Top with an additional sheet of phyllo; brush lightly with the melted butter. Place one cooked breast parallel to and about 3 inches from the bottom of the phyllo sheets, centering it. Fold about 3 inches of the long sides of the phyllo over the breast and toward the center; fold the bottom 3 inches over the breast. Roll the breast up to the top of the phyllo to form a packet. Place on the prepared baking sheet. Repeat with the remaining phyllo and breasts. Brush lightly with the melted butter. The dish can be made ahead to this point and refrigerated, covered, for several hours, until ready to serve.

Preheat the oven to 425°F. Bake the chilled phyllo bundles, uncovered, for 12 to 15 minutes or until well browned. Meanwhile, heat the wine-apple mixture in a medium saucepan over medium-high heat. When boiling, add the cream and continue to boil until reduced slightly, 3 to 4 minutes. When the phyllo bundles are browned, divide the sauce among four plates. Top with the phyllo bundles and serve.

✳

TRUC:

WHEN WORKING WITH PHYLLO, MAKE SURE TO KEEP THE SHEETS COVERED WITH A BARELY DAMP TOWEL UNTIL YOU USE THEM. PHYLLO DRIES VERY QUICKLY; COVERING IT KEEPS IT PLIABLE.

ESCALOPES DE VOLAILLE AU PARMESAN

CHICKEN SCALOPPINE WITH PARMESAN

Parmesan and basil perk up the standard flour dredging on these lovely chicken scaloppine. Moist and succulent, they make an elegantly easy, quickly prepared, after-work main course. Serve with sliced fresh tomatoes and spinach pasta tossed with olive oil and garlic.

MAKES **4** SERVINGS

Four 6- to 8-ounce boneless, skinless chicken
   breasts, tenderloin portions removed
5 ounces freshly grated Parmigiano-Reggiano
   cheese (about 1¼ cups)
¼ cup all-purpose flour
1 tablespoon chopped fresh basil
2 large egg whites
2 tablespoons olive oil
⅛ teaspoon freshly ground pepper

Lay each breast flat on a cutting board; cut in half horizontally to form two thin pieces; set aside. Stir the cheese and flour together in a shallow bowl; stir in the basil. Set aside. Stir the egg whites and 1 tablespoon water together in a shallow bowl with a fork until slightly foamy; set aside.

Heat 1 tablespoon of the olive oil in a large nonstick skillet over medium heat. When hot, working quickly, dip 4 breast pieces, one piece at a time, into the egg white mixture, then into the cheese mixture, turning to coat. Add to the hot skillet. Cook until browned and cooked through, 2 to 3 minutes per side. Remove to a platter; cover with aluminum foil to keep warm. Add the remaining 1 tablespoon of olive oil to the skillet; repeat with the remaining pieces of chicken. Season with pepper and serve.

✳

TRUC:

BUY THE BEST-QUALITY PARMESAN, PREFERABLY AUTHENTIC PARMIGIANO-REGGIANO, YOU CAN AFFORD AND GRATE IT FRESH JUST BEFORE USING FOR OPTIMUM TASTE.

PAELLA

---

*P*aella *is a common item in small restaurants close to the Spanish border but it is also available in almost any French market. Lined up with all the meat, cheese, and produce vendors is the paella seller. He takes his scoop and parcels out quantities of piping hot rice, chicken, and seafood into a plastic container from his giant paella pan. If your timing is right, you can take it home after shopping and enjoy it for lunch with a nice tossed salad made with market greens. Making it from scratch always produces the best results. Invite company to share some; it's almost impossible to make a small quantity. Pour your guests a glass of wine and have everyone join in the preparation.*

MAKES 6 SERVINGS

2 tablespoons olive oil

1 medium onion, chopped (about ¾ cup)

4 boneless, skinless chicken thighs,
  cut into thirds

½ pound chorizo sausage links, cut into
  2-inch pieces

1 medium red bell pepper, finely chopped

2 garlic cloves, minced

2 medium tomatoes, chopped

1½ cups Bomba, Arborio, or medium-grain rice

¾ teaspoon saffron, crumbled

½ teaspoon salt

¾ pound raw shelled and deveined
  medium shrimp

6 mussels, scrubbed and debearded

1 cup sugar snap peas

Heat the olive oil in a paella pan or large skillet over medium-high heat. When hot, add the onion; cook until beginning to soften, stirring frequently, 2 to 3 minutes. Add the chicken and sausage; cook until lightly browned, 4 to 5 minutes.

Add the bell pepper and garlic; stir to combine. Add the tomatoes; cook until they release their juices, 4 to 5 minutes. Stir in the rice.

Meanwhile, bring 4 cups (3 cups if using medium-grain rice) of water to a boil in a saucepan. Add the saffron to ½ cup of the boiling water; stir to dissolve. Add the remaining water to the rice mixture in the pan along with the dissolved saffron. Sprinkle with the salt; stir to combine. Boil for 5 minutes. Reduce the heat to low; cook for an additional 15 minutes. Add the shrimp, mussels, and peas; cook until the rice is tender and the seafood is cooked through, 8 to 10 minutes. Add additional water if all the liquid has evaporated before the rice is cooked through. Serve.

TRUC:

IF YOU CAN FIND IT, BUY BOMBA RICE FROM SPAIN TO MAKE THIS DISH. SIMILAR TO ARBORIO, THE RISOTTO RICE, BOMBA RICE SWELLS WITH MOISTURE BUT DOESN'T PRODUCE THE SAME CREAMINESS, MAKING IT A BETTER CHOICE FOR PAELLA. HOWEVER, EVEN MEDIUM-GRAIN REGULAR RICE WILL WORK. DIFFERENT TYPES OF RICE REQUIRE DIFFERENT AMOUNTS OF LIQUID, SO IT WILL BE NECESSARY TO ADJUST THE AMOUNT USED. ADD ANY ADDITIONAL WATER WHILE COOKING IN SMALL AMOUNTS; PAELLA SHOULD NOT BE SOUPY.

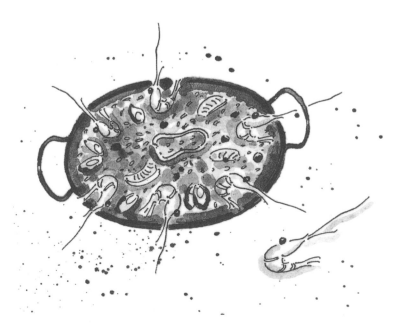

CHICKEN CUTLETS WITH CAPERS

Close relatives to escalopes, paillardes are pieces of meat that are pounded thin instead of sliced. Add a few capers, a little white wine, and fresh sage to the cooking pan for an "à la minute" sauce that transforms plain chicken into something special.

MAKES 4 SERVINGS

Four 5- to 6-ounce boneless, skinless chicken
  breasts, tenderloin sections removed
¼ teaspoon salt
¼ teaspoon freshly ground pepper
2 tablespoons olive oil
3 tablespoons butter
4 teaspoons capers, rinsed
2 tablespoons white wine
2 tablespoons minced fresh sage

Lay four sheets of plastic wrap or waxed paper on the counter; place a breast in the center of each sheet. Top each with another sheet of plastic wrap or waxed paper. Using a rolling pin or a meat mallet, flatten each breast to about ⅜-inch thickness to form paillardes. Blend the salt and pepper together in a small dish. Remove the top sheet from each paillarde; season with half the salt and pepper mixture. Heat 1 tablespoon of the olive oil and 1 tablespoon of the butter in a large skillet over medium-high heat. When sizzling, add two of the paillardes, using the remaining sheets of plastic wrap to lift them and flip them into the pan and peeling the plastic from the paillardes as they are added. Season the top of the paillardes with half the remaining salt and pepper mixture. Sauté them quickly until they are lightly browned on one side, 1 to 2 minutes;

turn and sauté on the other side until no longer
pink in the center when cut with a knife, 1 to 2
minutes. Remove to a platter; cover with
aluminum foil to keep warm. Add the remaining
1 tablespoon of olive oil to the skillet; when
hot, repeat the process with the remaining paillardes. Add to the platter and cover with foil.

Add the remaining 2 tablespoons of butter to
the skillet along with the capers. Quickly melt
and brown the butter, 1 to 2 minutes. Remove
from the heat and immediately add the white
wine and sage. Let the mixture bubble briefly,
swirling the pan to combine. Pour over the
paillardes and serve.

✳

TRUC:

CAPERS ARE SMALL BUDS PICKED FROM
BUSHES IN THE MEDITERRANEAN AND
PRESERVED. IF POSSIBLE, USE SALT-PACK
CAPERS INSTEAD OF THE BRINED VARIETY.
THEY HAVE A MORE SUBTLE TASTE. SOAK
THEM IN COLD WATER TO REMOVE SOME OF
THE SALTINESS; DRAIN AND USE. IF THEY
ARE UNAVAILABLE, MAKE SURE TO RINSE THE
BRINED CAPERS THOROUGHLY BEFORE USING.

CHICKEN-STUFFED VEGETABLES

The posted menus in each small French town are often variations on a theme. One chef may branch out here and there but often the listed offerings in any one town are remarkably similar. They reflect the specialties of that very specific area, what's seasonal, grown locally, and what's been eaten there for decades. That's not to say that going to a nearby town, you'll find the same items. You might, but frequently they will change to reflect another micro-territory—or terroir—of food and wine production.

Petits farcis, or stuffed small vegetables, seem to appear at every turn in the tiny restaurants of Old Nice. There, everything from little round zucchini to their golden blossoms is filled and baked or battered and fried. This recipe updates the process and is perfect for summer's peak produce, using the microwave to speed-cook the vegetables while the filling comes together.

MAKES 4 SERVINGS

1 medium red onion

1 medium yellow pepper

1 large tomato

1 medium zucchini (2¼ to 2½ inches in diameter)

1 tablespoon olive oil

2 teaspoons minced garlic

1 cup chopped cooked chicken

¼ teaspoon salt

⅛ teaspoon freshly ground pepper

⅓ cup garlic and herb cheese, such as Boursin
   or Alouette

2 tablespoons chopped fresh basil plus
   4 leaves for garnish

Cut the top third from the red onion, yellow pepper, and tomato. Cut a lengthwise strip from the zucchini at about one-third of its width. Reserve the onion top and zucchini strip for another use. Using a melon ball scoop or grapefruit spoon, scoop out the flesh of the onion and zucchini to within slightly more than ¼ inch of the sides and bottom, reserving the removed portions. Seed and core the yellow pepper. Juice and core the tomato, reserving the removed portion. Place the onion, yellow pepper, and zucchini on a microwave-safe plate. Microwave on high for 6 to 7 minutes, adding the tomato during the last 1½ minutes or until the vegetables are crisp-tender.

Meanwhile, chop the removed portion of the onion, the top portion of the yellow pepper, minus the stem, the removed portion of the zucchini, and the tomato flesh. Heat the olive oil in a large, nonstick skillet over medium heat. When hot, add the chopped onion and yellow pepper; sauté until tender, 4 to 5 minutes. Add the chopped zucchini and the garlic; sauté until fragrant, 30 seconds to 1 minute. Add the chopped tomato, including any juice, and cook until all the liquid has evaporated, about 2 minutes. Stir in the chicken, salt, and pepper; cook until heated through, about 1 minute. Remove from the heat; stir in the cheese and the chopped basil. Mound into the microwaved vegetables; garnish each with a basil leaf. To serve, bring to the table and cut each vegetable into quarters, serving one-quarter of each per person.

TRUCS:

MICROWAVES VARY SUBSTANTIALLY IN POWER FROM THE TINY DORM-ROOM VERSIONS TO THE NEW, HIGH-WATT MICROWAVES THAT COOK MUCH FASTER. THE BEST RULE IS TO CHECK FREQUENTLY SO AS TO NOT OVERCOOK.

EVER WONDER WHAT THAT PHRASE "RESERVE FOR ANOTHER USE" IS REALLY SUPPOSED TO MEAN? MOST OFTEN IT MEANS ENCASE IN PLASTIC WRAP AND PLACE IN THE BACK OF THE REFRIGERATOR TO KEEP ALL THE OTHER LEFTOVER BITS COMPANY. THE TRICK IS TO KEEP TRACK OF THESE ODDS AND ENDS AND USE THEM UP QUICKLY. THE STRIPS OF ZUCCHINI AND ONION IN THIS RECIPE EASILY INCORPORATE INTO OTHER RECIPES; JUST CHOP THE SCRAPS AND ADD TO SOUPS, OMELETS, SALADS, OR STEWS.

POULET À LA CATALANE
CATALAN CHICKEN

Most people familiar with the Catalan region associate it with Spain but it begins in southernmost France. The region extends from the area around Perpignan along piercingly blue Mediterranean beaches and over the hilly beginnings of the Pyrénées into Spain. As you drive through the region, you will see road signs in both French and Catalan, a tribute to two separate languages and cultures.

MAKES 4 SERVINGS

1 medium lemon

¼ cup all-purpose flour

½ teaspoon salt

⅛ teaspoon cayenne

4 bone-in, skin-on chicken thighs

2 bone-in, skin-on chicken breasts, cut in half crosswise across the bone

2 tablespoons olive oil

½ cup diced Serrano ham or prosciutto

½ cup white wine

8 whole garlic cloves, peeled

1 cup shelled fresh peas or 1 cup frozen and thawed peas

¼ cup sliced almonds

Slice the end from the lemon; cut 4 additional thin slices for garnish; set aside. Juice the remaining lemon; set aside.

Stir the flour, salt, and cayenne together in a shallow bowl; dredge the chicken pieces in the mixture.

Heat the olive oil in a large skillet over medium-high heat. When hot, add the chicken pieces; cook until well browned on both sides, 4 to 5 minutes per side. Reduce the heat to low; add the ham, white wine, garlic cloves, and reserved lemon juice. Cover; cook for 20 minutes. Turn and cook, covered, until the thighs are no longer pink in the thickest portion when cut with a knife, 15 to 20 minutes. Add the peas during the last 10 minutes of cooking time. To prepare ahead up to the point of adding the peas, when the chicken is cooked through, refrigerate, covered, until just before serving. Return to the skillet; heat over medium heat and add the peas while rewarming.

To serve, divide the chicken, peas, and pan juices among four plates. Sprinkle with the sliced almonds; garnish with the lemon slices.

✳

TRUC:

CUTTING CHICKEN BREASTS ACROSS THE BONE ALLOWS EVERYONE TO HAVE BOTH WHITE AND DARK MEAT AND ENJOY THE INTERPLAY OF DIFFERENT TEXTURES EACH PROVIDES. USE A HEAVY, SHARP KNIFE, POULTRY SHEARS, OR A CLEAVER TO CUT THROUGH THE BONE.

TARRAGON CHICKEN

Of all the herb choices possible with chicken, the French seem to love tarragon most of all. Thyme is a close rival but tarragon leads the list. Tarragon chicken, laced with cream, pops up everywhere; here it's done stovetop with chicken pieces for maximum flavor but variations include using boneless, skinless chicken breasts or cooking the dish as a stew. All produce a lush, subtly licorice-laced result that is irresistible.

MAKES 4 SERVINGS

1 tablespoon canola oil

1 tablespoon salted butter

4 bone-in, skin-on chicken thighs

2 bone-in, skin-on chicken breasts, cut in half crosswise across the bone

½ teaspoon salt

⅛ teaspoon freshly ground pepper

⅓ cup chopped shallots

½ cup white wine

1½ tablespoons chopped fresh tarragon

½ cup heavy cream

1 teaspoon sherry vinegar

Heat the canola oil and butter in a large skillet over medium heat. When sizzling, add the chicken pieces, seasoned with the salt and pepper, skin side down. Sauté until well browned, 4 to 5 minutes. Sprinkle with the shallots; turn and sauté until well browned, 4 to 5 minutes. Reduce the heat to low; add the white wine and sprinkle with ½ tablespoon of the tarragon. Cover; cook for 20 minutes. Turn and cook, covered, until the thighs are no longer pink in the thickest portion when cut with a knife, 15 to 20 minutes. Remove to a platter, skin side up; cover with aluminum foil to keep warm.

Stir the cream and sherry vinegar together in a small bowl; the cream will thicken. Whisk the cream mixture into the pan juices; increase the heat to medium-high and cook briefly to thicken, 1 to 2 minutes. Pour over the chicken; sprinkle with the remaining 1 tablespoon of tarragon.

TRUC:

TO SPEED COOKING TIMES, USE 4 BONELESS, SKINLESS CHICKEN BREASTS INSTEAD OF CHICKEN PIECES. AFTER ADDING THE WINE AND TARRAGON, COOK THE BREASTS FOR 4 TO 5 MINUTES PER SIDE, THEN REMOVE AND FINISH THE RECIPE AS INDICATED.

POULET NORMAND

NORMAN CHICKEN

The stone-arched entryway to rue de l'Exposition announces that this street is special. Just one block long and tucked in the shadow of the Eiffel Tower, it is home to several charming restaurants and bistros. I came to know one well when my friend Marie-Alice Beraud owned La Serre. It typified the slightly retrospective, funky atmosphere of the true Parisian bistro with lace curtains and toasters between tables used to heat Poilâne bread to the proper temperature for topping with foie gras. While Mir, her dog, snuggled in his basket behind the bar, she made dishes like Poulet Normand for locals.

MAKES 4 SERVINGS

1 tablespoon canola oil

1 tablespoon butter

4 bone-in, skin-on chicken thighs

2 bone-in, skin-on chicken breasts, cut in half crosswise across the bone

½ teaspoon salt

⅛ teaspoon pepper

⅓ cup Calvados, applejack, or brandy

½ cup hard cider

½ cup heavy cream

2 cooking apples, such as Granny Smith or Golden Delicious

Heat the canola oil and butter in a large skillet over medium heat. When sizzling, add the chicken pieces, seasoned with the salt and pepper. Sauté until golden brown on both sides, 3 to 4 minutes per side. Add the Calvados and immediately light with a match to flame. When the flames disappear, reduce the heat to low; add the cider and cream. Cover; cook for 20 minutes. Turn and cook, covered, until the thighs are no longer pink in the thickest portion when cut with a knife, 15 to 20 minutes.

Meanwhile, peel the apples; cut into 1-inch-wide slices. Add to the chicken during the last 10 minutes of cooking time. When the chicken is cooked through, remove the pieces along with the apple slices to a platter. Cover with aluminum foil to keep warm. (To prepare ahead to this point, refrigerate, covered, until just before serving. Return the chicken to the skillet; reheat gently over low heat. When heated through, remove to a platter and proceed.)

Increase the heat to high; boil the sauce until thickened slightly, 2 to 3 minutes. Pour over the chicken and apples and serve.

✳

TRUCS:

THE FRENCH MAKE, BOTTLE, AND SERVE HARD CIDER IN THE SAME FASHION AS WINE. IN THIS COUNTRY, HARD CIDER IS MORE OFTEN PREPARED AND SERVED ENGLISH STYLE, LIKE BEER, AND WORKS WELL AS A SUBSTITUTE. IF YOU WISH TO AVOID USING ALCOHOL, ELIMINATE THE STEP OF FLAMING WITH CALVADOS. SUBSTITUTE NONALCOHOLIC CIDER OR APPLE JUICE FOR THE HARD CIDER.

NOT ALL APPLES WORK WELL FOR COOKING. FOR EXAMPLE, THE GOLDEN DELICIOUS VARIETY HOLDS UP NICELY WHEN HEATED BUT RED DELICIOUS APPLES TURN TO MUSH. GRANNY SMITH APPLES ARE ANOTHER READILY AVAILABLE TYPE THAT WOULD WORK WELL IN THIS RECIPE.

CRISPY CHICKEN

---

*C*risp *on the outside, juicy inside, this chicken dish beats Colonel Sanders any day. For a lovely twist, omit the final wine reduction and pack the pieces in a picnic hamper with a chilled bottle of white Sancerre. Pretend you're dining along the banks of the Loire with châteaux scattered as a backdrop in the distance.*

MAKES 4 SERVINGS

½ teaspoon salt

¼ teaspoon dried thyme

⅛ teaspoon freshly ground pepper

4 bone-in, skin-on chicken thighs

2 bone-in, skin-on chicken breasts, cut in half crosswise across the bone

3 tablespoons clarified unsalted butter

½ cup white wine

Combine the salt, thyme, and pepper; season the chicken pieces with the mixture.

Heat the clarified butter in a large skillet over medium heat. When hot, add the chicken pieces, skin side down. Cook until just beginning to brown, 3 to 4 minutes. Reduce the heat to medium-low; cover and cook for 10 minutes. Remove the cover; turn and cook for an additional 10 minutes. Increase the heat to medium; turn again and cook until the skin is crisp and richly brown and the thighs are no longer pink in the thickest portion when cut with a knife, about 5 minutes. Remove to a platter; cover with aluminum foil to keep warm.

TRUC:

CLARIFY BUTTER TO KEEP IT FROM BURNING.
SIMPLY LET A STICK OF BUTTER MELT OVER
LOW HEAT UNTIL FOAMY. SKIM OFF THE
FOAM; POUR OR SPOON THE CLEAR, MELTED
LAYER OF BUTTERFAT UNDERNEATH INTO A
SMALL BOWL, LEAVING BEHIND THE MILKY
RESIDUE ON THE BOTTOM OF THE PAN.
CLARIFIED BUTTER WILL KEEP INDEFINITELY,
COVERED, IN THE REFRIGERATOR.

Pour off all but a small spoonful of accumulated
fat from the skillet; return to medium-high
heat. Add the white wine. Cook, scraping up
all brown bits on the bottom of the skillet,
until reduced to about 2 tablespoons, 2 to 3
minutes. Drizzle the wine reduction over the
chicken and serve.

ROCK CORNISH GAME HENS, TOAD STYLE

While checking a reference in my Larousse Gastronomique, *I found a full-color photo of a small chicken en crapaudine. Crapaud is the French word for toad and the picture strove to duplicate the namesake to the fullest. Not only was the little bird split lengthwise and flattened to make its shape resemble that of a toad, but peering up at me were two egg-white eyes with truffle pupils as well. I've skipped the eyeball garnish in this version but kept the shape, which lends itself to quick grilling.*

MAKES 4 SERVINGS

2 Rock Cornish game hens (about 1½ pounds each) or 2 poussins (about 1 pound each)

2 tablespoons Dijon mustard

2 teaspoons white wine vinegar

1 teaspoon ground ginger

1 teaspoon minced garlic

½ teaspoon salt

¼ teaspoon freshly ground pepper

2 tablespoons olive oil

Split the hens down the back, lengthwise, removing the spine. Remove the wing tips; reserve the spine and wing tips in the freezer for stock. Press the birds forward to crack the breastbone and then press down on the breast area to flatten. Rinse and pat dry. Mix the mustard, white wine vinegar, ginger, garlic, salt, and pepper together in a bowl until well blended; stir in the olive oil. Coat both sides of the hens with the mixture; let marinate while the grill heats.

Heat one side of a gas grill or mound coals on either side of a charcoal grill.

Grill the hens, skin side down, over medium-low heat, covered, on a gas grill or 4 to 6 inches over the coals on a charcoal grill until well browned, 5 to 8 minutes. Move to indirect heat and continue cooking for an additional 5 minutes, covered. Turn and cook, covered, over indirect heat until the juices run clear when the hens are cut with a knife between leg and thigh, 20 to 25 minutes. Remove to a platter. Bring the platter to the table; cut the hens in half lengthwise with poultry shears or a sharp knife. Serve.

TRUC:

POUSSINS, SMALL CHICKENS WEIGHING IN AT AROUND A POUND, CAN BE SPECIAL-ORDERED BUT ARE NOT READILY AVAILABLE. ROCK CORNISH GAME HENS ARE JUST SLIGHTLY LARGER AND CAN BE FOUND FROZEN, OR SOMETIMES FRESH, IN MOST MARKETS, MAKING THEM A PRACTICAL CHOICE. TO SPLIT THEM DOWN THE BACK, USE POULTRY SHEARS, A CLEAVER, OR A STURDY KNIFE. HOLD THE HEN VERTICALLY, BOTTOM END UP, AGAINST A CUTTING BOARD AND CUT ALONG THE SPINE ON EACH SIDE TO REMOVE. BECAUSE THE HENS ARE SO SMALL, THIS IS EASY TO DO.

GRILLED CHICKEN WITH HERBES DE PROVENCE

Small chickens have tender flesh that cooks quickly on the grill. In the hillsides around Provence, I love to eat at small restaurants and bistros that grill in hidden courtyards or cook in wood-burning ovens while patrons watch. Follow the smoky aroma they produce to locate them along sleepy winding streets and pathways.

MAKES 6 SERVINGS

¼ cup fresh lemon juice

¼ cup extra virgin olive oil

3½ teaspoons herbes de Provence

1 tablespoon minced garlic

Two 2½- to 2¾-pound small chickens, quartered

½ teaspoon salt

¼ teaspoon freshly ground pepper

Combine the lemon juice, olive oil, 3 teaspoons of the herbes de Provence, and the garlic in a large, self-sealing plastic bag. Add the chicken quarters; turn to coat. Marinate for 2 hours in the refrigerator. Heat both sides of a gas grill to medium-high heat or mound coals on one side of a charcoal grill and heat to medium-high heat. Turn off the flame on one side of the grill; remove the chicken quarters from the marinade and season with the salt and pepper. Discard the marinade. Place, skin side up, on the side without flame or coals. Cover the grill; cook, turning all pieces once, until the breasts are no longer pink in the thickest portion when cut with a knife, 15 to 20 minutes per side. Remove the breasts to a platter; cover with aluminum foil to keep warm. Turn the thigh pieces and cook until the juices are no longer pink when cut with a knife between the thigh and leg, about 10 minutes. Remove to the platter; sprinkle with the remaining ½ teaspoon herbes de Provence and serve.

TRUC:

IF POSSIBLE, BRIEFLY SOAK SOME DRIED HERB STALKS AND THROW THEM ON THE HEATED CERAMIC BRIQUETTES OR COALS TO LAYER AN ADDITIONAL SMOKED HERB FLAVOR ONTO THE CHICKENS.

SUPRÊMES DE VOLAILLE AUX OLIVES VERTES

CHICKEN BREASTS WITH GREEN OLIVES

Gnarled branches signal the presence of olives hiding behind silvery green leaves throughout Provence and the Côte d'Azur. The assertive flavor of picholine olives is the best choice for this dish. If they're unavailable, choose any imported green olive that isn't too bitter.

MAKES 4 SERVINGS

2 tablespoons olive oil

4 bone-in, skin-on chicken breasts

¼ teaspoon salt

¼ teaspoon freshly ground pepper

1 tablespoon minced garlic

¼ teaspoon crushed dried thyme

¼ cup Cognac

¾ cup white wine

½ cup pitted and coarsely chopped French
   picholine olives

8 ounces dried linguine noodles

Heat the olive oil in a large skillet over medium-high heat. When hot, add the breasts, seasoned with the salt and pepper, skin side down. Sauté until well browned, 4 to 5 minutes; turn and cook for an additional 5 to 7 minutes on the other side. Sprinkle with the garlic and thyme. Pour the Cognac over the breasts in the skillet; immediately light with a match to flame and cook until the flames disappear. Add the white wine and olives; reduce the heat to low. Cover; cook for 5 minutes; turn and cook until the breasts are no longer pink in the thickest portion when cut with a knife, about 10 minutes.

Meanwhile, cook the linguine according to the package directions. Drain well; divide among four dinner plates. Top each with a chicken breast; spoon the pan juices and olives over all.

TRUC:

FLATTEN OLIVES WITH THE SIDE OF A KNIFE BLADE TO EASILY REMOVE THE PIT.

POULETS AU FOUR

Roasts and Casseroles for Main Courses

CHICKEN BAECKOFFE

One of my favorite stops in Paris is Le Bec Rouge, a brasserie whose chef, Jean-Luc, does a cooking demonstration for my food tours and then feeds us copious amounts of the classic Alsatian casserole dish Baeckoffe afterward. My version is a bit lighter, using poultry instead of pork, but results in the same substantial presentation as the original.

MAKES 6 SERVINGS

½ small to medium head cabbage (about
   1 pound)

1 tablespoon olive oil

⅓ cup thick-cut smoked bacon strips (lardons),
   about ⅜ inch wide

4 bone-in, skin-on chicken thighs

2 bone-in, skin-on turkey thighs (see Truc)

1 bone-in, skin-on duck thigh and drumstick
   (cuisse), separated and well trimmed of fat

½ teaspoon salt

¼ teaspoon coarsely ground pepper

2 cups dry Alsatian Riesling wine

4 medium onions, cut into ¼-inch slices

6 medium Yukon Gold potatoes (about
   2 pounds), cut into ½-inch slices

6 crushed juniper berries

3 crushed garlic cloves

½ teaspoon dried thyme

1 bay leaf

1 cup reduced-sodium chicken broth

Preheat the oven to 325°F.

Fill a large pot two-thirds full of water; bring to a boil over medium-high heat. Add the cabbage and gently boil for 5 minutes; drain. When cool enough to handle, cut into ¾-inch slices; set aside.

Heat the olive oil in a large skillet over medium-high heat. When hot, add the lardons and sauté until well browned, 3 to 4 minutes. Remove to a deep, 4-quart oval baking dish (baeckoffe) or a Dutch oven. Add the poultry pieces, seasoned with the salt and pepper, in batches; sauté until very well browned on both sides, 5 to 6 minutes per side. Remove. Pour off any fat from the skillet. Add the wine to the skillet; simmer for a minute or two, scraping up any brown bits. Set aside.

To assemble, layer half the sliced onions over the lardons; layer half the potatoes over the onions. Top with the sliced cabbage, then the browned poultry pieces. Sprinkle with the juniper berries, garlic, and thyme. Add the bay leaf along the side of the baking dish. Layer the remaining onions over all; top with the remaining potatoes. Pour the reserved wine into the casserole; pour in the broth.

Bake, covered, for 1 hour; remove the cover and bake for an additional hour or until the poultry is fork tender. Remove the bay leaf before serving.

✳

TRUCS:

IF POSSIBLE, HAVE YOUR BUTCHER CUT EACH TURKEY THIGH IN HALF ACROSS THE BONE. IN FRANCE, THE TOPS OF TURKEY LEGS ARE CUT INTO DISKS AND MARKETED AS TURKEY OSSO BUCO. USING THIGHS CUT IN HALF PRODUCES SOMETHING SIMILAR. BOTH LEG AND THIGH PIECES BRAISE PARTICULARLY NICELY AND LEND THEMSELVES TO EXTENDED COOKING.

BLANCHING THE CABBAGE BEFORE ADDING IT TO THE BAECKOFFE TAMES ITS ASSERTIVENESS AND KEEPS IT FROM OVERWHELMING THE REST OF THE INGREDIENTS.

STUFFED CAPON WITH SWISS CHARD AND MUSHROOMS

A whole capon, like a turkey, has a festive air. Stuffed with dried fruits and wild mushrooms, this dressy main course offering enhances any holiday table. The succulent bird, sliced, sauced, and served with the filling on the side, needs little to accompany it besides good bread and, for an American touch, a wild rice pilaf.

MAKES 6 TO 8 SERVINGS

1 orange

½ cup chopped dried apricots

¼ cup raisins

1 ounce dried porcini mushrooms (cèpes)

2 tablespoons olive oil

1 large onion, chopped

2 teaspoons minced garlic

8 ounces white button mushrooms, chopped

1 bunch red Swiss chard (about 12 ounces),
   roughly chopped, including stems, or one 9-ounce
   package chopped frozen spinach, thawed

2 teaspoons chopped fresh rosemary

2 teaspoons fresh lemon thyme leaves or
   ¾ teaspoon dried thyme

¾ teaspoon salt

½ teaspoon freshly ground pepper

2 large eggs

1 tablespoon marc or Cognac, optional

One 7- to 8-pound capon

2 tablespoons salted butter, softened

2 cups reduced-sodium chicken broth

1 cup red wine

Grate the zest from the orange; reserve. Juice the orange. Soak the apricots and raisins with 2 tablespoons of the orange juice for 30 minutes; reserve the remaining juice for another use. Soak the porcini mushrooms in 2 cups of very hot water for 30 minutes; remove with a slotted spoon. Chop the porcini mushrooms. Strain the soaking liquid through a coffee filter; set aside.

Heat the olive oil in a large skillet over medium heat. When hot, add the onion; sauté until softened, 4 to 5 minutes. Add the garlic; sauté until fragrant, 30 seconds to 1 minute. Add the button mushrooms; sauté until the mushrooms are beginning to soften, 3 to 4 minutes. Add the apricots, raisins, orange juice, porcini mushrooms, half of the strained soaking liquid, and the chopped chard; cook, stirring often, until all the liquid has evaporated, about 10 minutes. Remove from the heat; stir in the reserved orange zest, the rosemary, lemon thyme, ½ teaspoon of the salt, and ¼ teaspoon of the pepper. Spoon into a shallow bowl to cool, stirring occasionally, 40 to 50 minutes. Whisk the eggs with the marc, if using, in a bowl; stir into the cooled chard mixture.

Meanwhile, preheat the oven to 325°F.

Stuff the cavity of the capon loosely with half of the mushroom stuffing; tie the legs of the capon together with kitchen twine. Place the remaining mushroom stuffing in a casserole; cover with aluminum foil and refrigerate until ready to bake. Rub the outer surface of the capon with the softened butter; season with the remaining ¼ teaspoon of salt and ¼ teaspoon of pepper. Place on a rack in a large, shallow roasting pan. Cover loosely with aluminum foil.

Bake the capon for 2 hours; remove the foil. Bake, along with the covered casserole of mushroom stuffing, for another 45 minutes to 1¼ hours, basting the capon occasionally, until the internal temperature of the stuffing inside the cavity reaches 165°F on a thermometer and the thermometer registers 180°F when inserted in the thickest portion of the thigh.

Meanwhile, place the broth, the remaining mushroom soaking liquid, and the red wine in a saucepan. Boil over medium-high heat until reduced to 1½ cups, about 20 minutes.

Let the capon rest for 10 minutes; untie the legs. Remove the stuffing from the cavity; add to the casserole. Degrease the roasting juices in the roasting pan; add the wine mixture to the pan. Bring to a boil over medium heat, scraping up any brown bits from the bottom of the pan. Strain into a pitcher. Carve the capon; serve with the stuffing. Spoon a small amount of the wine sauce over the capon; serve the remainder separately.

TRUC:

WITH TURKEY, BY THE TIME THE STUFFING IS HOT ENOUGH, THE BREAST MEAT IS DRIED OUT; THIS IS NOT TRUE WITH CAPON BECAUSE ITS MEAT IS SO MOIST.

CHICKEN BISTEEYA

*I*n *North Africa, home to the former French colonies of Algeria, Morocco, and Tunisia, pigeons fill this buttery, crisp creation, but chicken thighs work as well as their cooing cousins in the following interpretation.*

MAKES 6 SERVINGS

One 14-ounce can reduced-sodium chicken broth

1 cup chopped fresh parsley

½ cup chopped onions

8 tablespoons (1 stick) unsalted butter

2 tablespoons chopped fresh cilantro

3 cinnamon sticks

2 garlic cloves, smashed

2 teaspoons ras el hanout (see Truc)

1 teaspoon ground ginger

1 teaspoon freshly ground pepper

¼ teaspoon turmeric

1½ pounds boneless, skinless chicken thighs

¼ cup fresh lemon juice

10 eggs

8 ounces slivered almonds (about 2 cups)

2 tablespoons canola oil

⅓ cup confectioners' sugar

2 teaspoons ground cinnamon

Eight 17 × 12-inch leaves phyllo, thawed

¾ teaspoon salt

Combine the broth, ½ cup of water, the parsley, onions, 2 tablespoons of the butter, the cilantro, cinnamon sticks, garlic, ras el hanout, ginger, pepper, and turmeric in a large saucepan. Add the thighs and bring just to a boil over medium heat. Reduce the heat to low; simmer until the thighs are tender and no longer pink in the thickest portion when cut with a knife, 15 to 20 minutes. Remove the thighs and let cool briefly; dice and set aside. Remove the garlic cloves and cinnamon sticks from the cooking liquid. Bring the liquid to a boil over high heat and reduce to about 1¾ cups, 6 to 8 minutes. Add the lemon juice. Beat the eggs until foamy and whisk into the cooking liquid. Cook until the eggs form curds. Drain the curds in a strainer and reserve; discard the cooking liquid.

BISTRO CHICKEN **114**

salt. Top with the chopped almond mixture. Lay a sheet of phyllo over all. Fold in all the overhanging phyllo ends and brush with butter. Center the two last pieces of phyllo on top in a double layer and tuck under all around; brush with butter.

Bake for 15 minutes. Remove and invert onto a cookie sheet. Bake for an additional 10 minutes, until well browned and crisp. Invert onto a platter and serve.

Meanwhile, preheat the oven to 425°F.

Toss the almonds with the canola oil and toast on a shallow baking sheet until browned, about 5 minutes. Drain on paper towels and let cool. When cool, place in a food processor fitted with a metal blade; add the confectioners' sugar and ground cinnamon. Pulse to coarsely chop.

Melt the remaining 6 tablespoons of butter. Lay the phyllo sheets on the counter; keep covered with a damp cloth. Brush the bottom of a large, ovenproof skillet, paella pan, or tart pan lightly with the melted butter. Lay one sheet of phyllo over the pan; brush lightly with butter. Place one sheet of phyllo half in and half out of the pan; brush with butter. Repeat with three more sheets, layering half on and half off the pan, overlapping the sheets, and brushing each with butter. Scatter the diced chicken in an even layer over the bottom of the pan. Sprinkle with ¼ teaspoon of the salt. Top with the egg curds and sprinkle with the remaining ½ teaspoon of

TRUC:

RAS EL HANOUT IS A COMMON MOROCCAN SPICE BLEND, EASILY FOUND IN FRANCE BUT HARDER TO FIND HERE. IT CAN BE MAIL-ORDERED OR YOU CAN MAKE YOUR OWN QUICK VERSION. COMBINE 1 TEASPOON CURRY POWDER WITH ½ TEASPOON GROUND CORIANDER, ½ TEASPOON GROUND CUMIN, ¼ TEASPOON GROUND CINNAMON, AND ¼ TEASPOON ALLSPICE.

MARRAKECH CHICKEN

Rice, enhanced with spices, fills the chicken and perfumes its flesh. Since the cavity is small and the aroma so enticing, the recipe includes extra rice so no one is slighted.

MAKES 4 SERVINGS

4 tablespoons (½ stick) salted butter

1¼ teaspoons salt

1 cup raw long-grain rice

½ cup raisins

¼ cup slivered almonds

2 tablespoons confectioners' sugar

1 teaspoon ground cinnamon

1 teaspoon ras el hanout (see Truc, page 115)

¼ teaspoon ground ginger

¼ teaspoon freshly ground pepper

1 large onion, thickly sliced

One 3½- to 4-pound chicken

1 cup reduced-sodium chicken broth

Pinch saffron threads

Bring 3 cups of water, 1 tablespoon of the butter, and 1 teaspoon of the salt to a boil in a medium saucepan over medium-high heat. Stir in the rice; reduce the heat to low. Cook, covered, until the rice is just tender, about 20 minutes; drain. Place in a medium bowl; toss with 2 tablespoons of the butter. Stir in the raisins and almonds. Combine the confectioners' sugar, ¾ teaspoon of the cinnamon, ¾ teaspoon of the ras el hanout, the ginger, and ⅛ teaspoon of the pepper together in a small bowl; stir into the rice and set aside.

Meanwhile, preheat the oven to 375°F.

Scatter the onion slices in the center of a shallow roasting pan. Combine the remaining 1 tablespoon of butter, ¼ teaspoon of salt, ¼ teaspoon of cinnamon, ¼ teaspoon of ras el hanout, and ⅛ teaspoon of pepper in a small bowl to form a paste. Rub the chicken with the butter mixture; place on top of the onion slices. Fill the chicken cavity with 1¼ cups of the rice mixture; reserve the remainder. Heat 1 cup of water and ½ cup of the broth in a small saucepan; add the saffron and stir to dissolve. Pour into the roasting pan. Roast for 1 hour 30 minutes to 1 hour 40 minutes, basting occasionally, or until a thermometer registers 165°F when inserted into the center of the rice. Remove to a platter.

Add the remaining ½ cup of broth to the roasting pan; bring to a simmer over medium-low heat, scraping up any roasting juices and brown bits. Strain into a small bowl; use a spoon to degrease any fat and serve with the chicken.

Meanwhile, place the reserved rice in a medium saucepan with ¼ cup water; cover and cook until heated through, 3 to 4 minutes. Serve with the chicken.

✳

TRUC:
USE COOKED COUSCOUS INSTEAD OF RICE FOR AN EQUALLY APPEALING STUFFING. PREPARE ¾ CUP OF COUSCOUS ACCORDING TO THE PACKAGE DIRECTIONS AND TOSS WITH THE 2 TABLESPOONS OF BUTTER, THE RAISINS, AND THE ALMONDS. PROCEED WITH THE RECIPE AS DIRECTED.

CASSEROLE-ROASTED CHICKEN

Baking a plump hen in a casserole provides just the right steamy atmosphere for cooking the firmer flesh of a larger fowl. Be careful, though, to choose a young bird. Watch out for tough skin and long hairs on a larger chicken; these are signs of age and the tougher flesh is more suitable for long stewing or for making stock.

In a bistro, the succulent, casserole-roasted bird would be served plated—sliced and drizzled with the pan juices. At home, try bringing the chicken out whole in all its glory and carve to order tableside.

MAKES 6 SERVINGS

One 4½- to 5½-pound chicken
2 tablespoons salted butter
1 medium onion, chopped
1 large carrot, chopped
1 celery stalk, chopped
½ teaspoon dried thyme
½ teaspoon salt
¼ teaspoon freshly ground pepper
1 tablespoon canola oil
¼ cup red or white wine

Preheat the oven to 325°F. Rinse the inner cavity of the chicken to remove any pooled blood and pat dry; set aside.

Heat 1 tablespoon of the butter in a large skillet over medium heat. When sizzling, add the onion, carrot, and celery; sauté until the onion begins to soften, 4 to 5 minutes. Remove from the heat; stir in ¼ teaspoon of the thyme, ¼ teaspoon of the salt, and ⅛ teaspoon of the pepper. Set aside ½ cup of the vegetable mixture; place the remainder in the bottom of a large Dutch oven or a heavy, lidded, ovenproof casserole deep enough to hold the chicken.

Heat the canola oil in the skillet. When hot, place the chicken in the skillet breast side down; sauté until golden brown, 3 to 4 minutes.

Gently turn with tongs, taking care not to break the skin, and sauté the back until golden brown, 3 to 4 minutes. Ease the chicken onto one side and sauté until golden brown, 3 to 4 minutes; repeat with the other side. Remove from the heat and transfer the chicken to the Dutch oven, breast side up. Spoon the reserved ½ cup of vegetables into the chicken cavity. Melt the remaining 1 tablespoon of butter in the skillet; stir in the remaining ¼ teaspoon of thyme, ¼ teaspoon of salt, and ⅛ teaspoon of pepper, scraping the bottom of the skillet to incorporate any brown bits. Pour the melted butter mixture over the chicken; cover with a tight-fitting lid. Bake until a thermometer registers 180°F when inserted in the thickest portion of the thigh and the juices run clear, about 1½ hours.

Remove the chicken to a platter; cover with aluminum foil to keep warm. Strain the vegetables from the cooking juices. Degrease the cooking juices and pour into a saucepan. Add the wine; bring to a boil over high heat. Boil to reduce slightly, 2 to 3 minutes; serve in a pitcher with the chicken.

✳

TRUCS:

INSTANT-READ THERMOMETERS GIVE ACCURATE RESULTS QUICKLY AND EASILY. THEY CAN BE PURCHASED IN ALMOST ANY COOKWARE STORE OR DEPARTMENT.

FOR A NOUVELLE CUISINE TOUCH, PLACE THE STRAINED VEGETABLES IN A BLENDER. ADD THE WINE TO THE COOKING JUICES, COOLING THE LIQUID SLIGHTLY, AND ADD TO THE BLENDER. PURÉE AND POUR INTO A SAUCEPAN. BRING TO A BOIL OVER MEDIUM HEAT AND GENTLY BOIL FOR SEVERAL MINUTES TO BLEND THE FLAVORS. THIS TECHNIQUE OF USING THE COOKING VEGETABLES AS A THICKENER IS VERY COMMON IN NOUVELLE CUISINE.

Chicken with Garlic

Roasting the garlic with the chicken develops the cloves into mellow, soft pods of spreadable goodness. Squeeze the garlic out of the roasted cloves and slather it onto slices of French bread.

MAKES 4 SERVINGS

2 large heads garlic, broken into cloves, unpeeled

One 3½- to 4-pound chicken

1 teaspoon dried thyme

¼ teaspoon salt

¼ teaspoon freshly ground pepper

1 tablespoon olive oil

½ lemon

1 sprig rosemary

1 cup white wine

1 cup reduced-sodium chicken broth

Preheat the oven to 375°F.

Scatter the garlic cloves over the bottom of a medium-sized, shallow roasting pan. Rinse the inner cavity of the chicken to remove any pooled blood; pat dry. Place the chicken on a rack in the roasting pan. Combine the thyme, salt, and pepper; sprinkle the chicken outside and inside the cavity with the seasoning. Rub the outside with the olive oil. Place the lemon and rosemary in the chicken cavity. Pour the white wine and broth into the bottom of the pan. Roast for 1 hour 20 minutes to 1½ hours or until a thermometer registers 180°F when inserted in the thickest portion of the thigh and the juices run clear. Remove the chicken to a platter; surround with cloves of garlic.

Place the pan juices in a small bowl; use a spoon to degrease any fat and serve with the chicken.

✳

TRUC:

IF THERE ARE LEFTOVER CLOVES OF ROASTED GARLIC, SQUEEZE OUT THE INTERIOR AND REFRIGERATE, WELL COVERED, TO INCORPORATE INTO MASHED POTATOES, SALAD DRESSINGS, PIZZA SAUCES, OR INTO GOAT CHEESE FOR AN APPETIZER SPREAD.

CHICKEN BAKED WITH COMTÉ CHEESE

Comté is the French answer to Swiss Gruyère and in fact is sometimes labeled Comté-Gruyère. With a lineage that dates back to the thirteenth century, this cow's milk cheese has a long tradition of use in many recipes. One classic pairing is the following.

MAKES 4 SERVINGS

¾ cup reduced-sodium chicken broth

½ cup heavy cream

2 teaspoons Dijon mustard

⅛ teaspoon grated nutmeg

1 tablespoon canola oil

1 chicken, cut into 8 pieces (see Note)

¼ teaspoon salt

⅛ teaspoon freshly ground pepper

½ cup white wine

4 ounces grated Comté or Swiss Gruyère cheese
  (about 1 cup)

2 tablespoons all-purpose flour

Preheat the oven to 375°F. Add the broth, cream, mustard, and nutmeg to the bottom of a shallow 2-quart baking dish; whisk to combine.

Heat the canola oil in a large skillet over medium-high heat. When hot, brown the chicken, seasoned with the salt and pepper, in batches; sauté until golden brown on both sides, 3 to 4 minutes per side. Remove. Drain any fat from the skillet. Add ¼ cup of the white wine, scraping up any brown bits from the bottom of the skillet; pour into the baking dish. Top with the browned chicken pieces in a single layer.

Note: For 8 pieces, purchase a cut-up chicken and cut the breasts in half crosswise across the bone. Reserve the wings for later use. To cut up a whole chicken yourself, remove the thigh and drumstick portions; separate the thighs from the drumsticks. Remove the back portion and reserve in the freezer to make broth and stock. Separate the whole breast portion into two halves along the breast bone and then cut each breast into two portions, French style. Cut across the bone, cutting the bottom portion about two-thirds of the way up. Leave the wing attached to the upper third portion.

TRUC:

THANKS TO THE BURGEONING POPULARITY OF QUALITY CHEESE, IT IS BECOMING EASIER TO FIND SELECTIONS SUCH AS COMTÉ. IF UNAVAILABLE IN YOUR MARKET, REPLACE IT WITH EITHER OF ITS CLOSE COUSINS, GRUYÈRE OR THE LARGER-HOLED EMMENTALER FROM SWITZERLAND.

Bake for 40 to 45 minutes, until the thighs are no longer pink in the thickest portion when cut with a knife. Remove the chicken; pour the cooking liquid into a saucepan. Return the chicken to the baking dish; top with the grated cheese. Change the oven temperature to broil; broil with the chicken in the center of the oven for 5 minutes, until the cheese is crusty and browned.

Meanwhile, skim off any fat from the cooking liquid; bring to a boil over medium-high heat. Whisk together the flour and the remaining ¼ cup of white wine; whisk into the boiling liquid. Boil until slightly thickened, 1 to 2 minutes. When the cheese is crusty, pour the sauce into the bottom of the baking dish and serve.

CHICKEN WITH GARLIC CROUTONS

Croutes, or, as we call them, croutons, are crisp, browned slices of French bread. Permeated with garlic-flavored olive oil and pan juices, they gild the simple salad garnish to this roast chicken.

MAKES 4 SERVINGS

One 3½- to 4-pound chicken

1 cup reduced-sodium chicken broth

½ cup white wine

3 tablespoons olive oil

8 whole medium garlic cloves, peeled

Six ½-inch-thick slices stale baguette, cut in half

¼ teaspoon dried thyme

¼ teaspoon salt

⅛ teaspoon freshly ground pepper

8 cups torn romaine lettuce

Preheat the oven to 375°F.

Rinse the inner cavity of the chicken to remove any pooled blood; pat dry. Place the chicken on a rack in a medium-sized, shallow roasting pan. Pour the broth and white wine into the bottom of the pan. Heat the olive oil in a large skillet over low heat. Add the garlic and gently cook, turning several times, for 10 minutes. Remove the garlic cloves and place in the chicken cavity. Increase the heat to medium-high; add the baguette pieces. Sauté, turning once halfway through, until browned and crisp, about 5 minutes total. Place in the chicken cavity.

Drizzle the olive oil remaining in the skillet over the chicken; rub to coat. Season with the thyme, salt, and pepper. Roast for 1 hour 20 minutes to 1½ hours or until a thermometer registers 180°F when inserted in the thickest portion of the thigh and the juices run clear. Remove the chicken to a platter.

Put the romaine in a salad bowl; remove the garlic and croutons from the chicken cavity and add to the romaine; toss with ¼ cup of the hot pan juices. Serve the salad with the chicken. Serve the remaining pan juices on the side.

TRUC:

SINCE GARLIC BURNS EASILY, MAKE SURE TO COOK IT WITH THE OLIVE OIL OVER VERY LOW HEAT. IF NECESSARY, MOVE THE SKILLET ON AND OFF THE BURNER TO SLOW THE PROCESS. THIS GENTLE POACHING INFUSES THE OLIVE OIL WITH A MELLOW GARLIC FLAVOR THAT TRANSFERS TO THE CROUTONS WHEN THEY ARE SAUTÉED.

POULET AU GENIÈVRE

CHICKEN WITH JUNIPER BERRIES

Juniper, ginger, and coriander seeds often complement wild fowl but spark woodsy notes in domestic poultry as well. In the fall, menus showcase treatments like this throughout France in honor of la chasse *(the hunt). Our urban alternative to foraging is the butcher case, offering cut-up chickens 24/7.*

MAKES 4 SERVINGS

½ teaspoon salt

½ teaspoon juniper berries, crushed

⅛ teaspoon coriander seeds, crushed

⅛ teaspoon freshly ground pepper

1 tablespoon canola oil

2 ounces salt pork, rind removed, cut into strips (lardons; about ⅓ cup)

One 3½- to 4-pound chicken, cut into 8 pieces (see Note, page 123)

1 medium carrot, chopped

1 small onion, chopped

1 cup white wine

¼ cup heavy cream

2 tablespoons gin

2 teaspoons cornstarch

Preheat the oven to 375°F. Combine the salt, juniper berries, coriander seeds, and pepper; set aside.

Heat the canola oil in a large skillet over medium-high heat. When hot, add the lardons; sauté until browned, 4 to 5 minutes. Remove with a slotted spoon to a Dutch oven. Add the chicken, in batches; sauté until well browned on both sides, 4 to 5 minutes per side. Remove to the Dutch oven, layering the breast pieces on top of the drumsticks and thighs. Add the carrot and onion; sauté until just beginning to soften, 2 to 3 minutes. Remove with a slotted spoon; scatter over the chicken. Sprinkle the juniper berry mixture over all. Pour off any fat from the skillet; add the white wine. Bring to a simmer, scraping up any brown bits from the bottom of the skillet; pour into the Dutch oven.

Bake for 50 to 60 minutes, until the thighs are
no longer pink in the thickest portion when cut
with a knife. Remove the chicken to a platter;
cover with foil to keep warm.

Strain the cooking juices into a saucepan; add
the cream and bring to a boil over high heat.
Boil until reduced by a third, about 5 minutes.
Stir the gin and cornstarch together; whisk into
the cooking juices. Boil until thickened and the
alcohol flavor of the gin has dissipated, 1 to 2
minutes. Pour the sauce over the chicken. Serve.

TRUC:

ADDING A SPLASH OF GIN AT THE END OF
COOKING ACCENTUATES AND FRESHENS THE
JUNIPER SEASONING. MAKE SURE TO BOIL
OFF THE ALCOHOL BEFORE SERVING OR
YOUR CHICKEN WILL TASTE LIKE IT JUST
FINISHED A MARTINI.

POULET AUX LENTILLES

CHICKEN WITH LENTILS

Lentils appear over and over again on bistro menus with petit salé—salt pork—*or with duck. Chicken thighs, quick-brined with seasonings, make a wonderful substitute. Serve this with a quick stir-fry of Savoy cabbage.*

MAKES 4 SERVINGS

⅓ cup coarse sea salt plus ¼ teaspoon salt

1 tablespoon sugar

15 juniper berries, coarsely chopped

1 tablespoon dried thyme

1 teaspoon coarsely ground pepper

⅛ teaspoon ground cloves

8 bone-in, skin-on chicken thighs

2 cups lentils

1-pound package baby carrots

1 cup frozen baby onions, thawed

1 tablespoon minced garlic

½ cup white wine

Stir together the sea salt, sugar, juniper berries, 1½ teaspoons of the thyme, ½ teaspoon of the pepper, and the cloves. Place the chicken thighs in a single layer in a nonreactive container; sprinkle on both sides with the salt mixture. Rub into the thighs. Refrigerate, covered, for 4 to 6 hours to brine. Rinse under cold water; pat dry.

Preheat the oven to 325°F. Cook the lentils with 5 cups of water in a large saucepan until just beginning to be tender, about 20 minutes; drain. Place in the bottom of a 13 × 9-inch glass or ceramic baking dish. Top with the carrots and onions. Combine the garlic, the remaining 1½ teaspoons of thyme, ½ teaspoon of pepper, and ¼ teaspoon of salt in a small dish; sprinkle over all. Top with the chicken thighs. Add 2 cups of water and the white wine to the baking dish. Bake for 2 hours or until the chicken is fork tender, the lentils have softened, and almost all the cooking liquid is gone.

✳

TRUCS:

INSTEAD OF A SALTWATER SOLUTION TO BRINE THE THIGHS, A HERB-SALT RUB PROVIDES A SIMILAR EFFECT.

IF AVAILABLE, USE FRENCH LENTILS FROM PUY TO ADD AUTHENTICITY; OTHERWISE, REGULAR BROWN LENTILS ARE PERFECTLY SATISFACTORY.

CHICKEN BRINED WITH SPICES

*M*oist and lightly infused with mustard, spices, and wine, this variation on a poulet rôti is a great way to boost flavor in a non–free-range, supermarket bird.

MAKES 4 SERVINGS

½ cup coarse sea salt

8 garlic cloves, crushed

3 tablespoons Dijon mustard

4 cloves

2 cinnamon sticks

½ teaspoon black peppercorns

1 cup white wine

One 3½- to 4-pound chicken

1 medium onion, thickly sliced

1 tablespoon salted butter, softened

Put the salt, garlic, mustard, cloves, cinnamon, and peppercorns in a large saucepan. Add 5 cups of water and the white wine; stir to blend. Bring the mixture to a boil over medium-high heat, stirring often. Remove from the heat and let cool to room temperature, about 2 hours. Rinse the inner cavity of the chicken to remove any pooled blood; place the chicken in a large, self-sealing plastic bag. Pour the marinade over the chicken. Squeeze the bag to remove all excess air, bringing the brine up and around the chicken to cover. Refrigerate for 4 to 6 hours.

TRUC:

FOR AN EASY ACCOMPANIMENT, SCATTER
YUKON GOLD POTATOES, CUT IN CHUNKS,
AROUND THE CHICKEN DURING THE LAST 45
MINUTES TO AN HOUR OF ROASTING.

Preheat the oven to 375°F.

Place the onion slices in the bottom of a
medium-sized, shallow roasting pan. Remove
the chicken from the marinade and pat dry.
Discard the marinade. Rub the chicken with
the butter and place on top of the onion slices.
Roast for 1 hour 20 minutes to 1 hour 40
minutes or until a thermometer reaches 180°F
when inserted in the thickest portion of the
thigh and the juices run clear. Remove the
chicken to a platter, surround with the onions,
and serve.

Chicken with Morel Mushrooms

I eat this luscious chicken and think of wood-paneled walls sealing out the sound of Parisian traffic. I see carefully set tables and hear muted dinner conversation and am transported back to the Auberge Bressane on avenue de la Motte-Piquet with every forkful of this dish they do so well.

MAKES 4 SERVINGS

2 tablespoons canola oil

1 tablespoon butter

One 3½- to 4-pound cut-up chicken

½ teaspoon salt

⅛ teaspoon freshly ground pepper

½ cup chopped shallots

8 ounces white button mushrooms, sliced

4 ounces morel mushrooms, well rinsed
  and quartered

¼ cup Cognac

⅔ cup white wine

⅔ cup heavy cream

4 sprigs parsley

2 sprigs thyme

2 teaspoons cornstarch

Preheat the oven to 350°F.

Heat 1 tablespoon of the canola oil and the butter in a large skillet over medium-high heat. When hot, add the chicken, seasoned with the salt and pepper, in batches; sauté until well browned on both sides, 4 to 5 minutes per side. Remove. Put the remaining 1 tablespoon of canola oil in the skillet with the shallots; sauté for 1 minute. Add the button mushrooms and the morels; sauté until the button mushrooms are tender, 4 to 5 minutes. Return the chicken to the skillet; pour the Cognac over the chicken. Immediately light with a match to flame and cook until the flames disappear. Put the chicken, mushrooms, and any pan juices in a Dutch oven. Pour the white wine into the skillet; bring to a simmer, scraping up any brown bits on the bottom of the skillet. Stir in the cream; pour into the Dutch oven. Add the sprigs of parsley and thyme. Cover; bake for 1¼ hours or until the chicken thighs are no longer pink in the thickest portion when cut with a knife. Remove the chicken and mushrooms to a platter, discarding the parsley and thyme; cover with aluminum foil to keep warm.

Bring the cooking liquid to a boil over high heat. Stir 3 tablespoons of water and the cornstarch together; slowly whisk into the liquid. Boil until slightly thickened, 1 to 2 minutes. Pour over the chicken and serve.

TRUC:

IF FRESH MORELS ARE NOT AVAILABLE, SUBSTITUTE ½ OUNCE DRIED MORELS. SOAK THEM IN 1 CUP OF HOT WATER OR CHICKEN BROTH IN A MEDIUM BOWL FOR 30 MINUTES OR UNTIL SOFTENED. REMOVE THE RECONSTITUTED MORELS WITH A SLOTTED SPOON AND QUARTER THEM. ADD THE MORELS TO THE SKILLET AS DIRECTED. STRAIN THE SOAKING LIQUID THROUGH A COFFEE FILTER TO REMOVE ANY GRIT; ADD THE STRAINED LIQUID TO THE MUSHROOM MIXTURE IN THE SKILLET. COOK UNTIL ALL THE LIQUID HAS EVAPORATED. PROCEED WITH THE RECIPE AS DIRECTED.

CLASSIC ROAST CHICKEN WITH FRIES

Order a roast chicken from any bistro menu and you know exactly what you're getting. Brown and glistening, garnished with piping hot fries, a quarter section of poultry perfection awaits knife, fork, and un verre of your favorite wine. A universal staple, from small cafés to trendy offshoots of three-star restaurants, poulet rôti is bistro cooking. Even better, roast chicken is easily duplicated at home. Include the fries if you wish, as they add a certain je ne sais quoi, but feel free to serve the chicken with another potato choice, such as mashed, for a simpler variation.

MAKES 4 SERVINGS

POULET RÔTI

One 3½- to 4-pound chicken

1½ teaspoons minced garlic

¼ teaspoon salt

2 tablespoons salted butter, softened

½ teaspoon dried thyme

¼ teaspoon freshly ground pepper

1 small onion, halved

1 cup white wine

1 cup reduced-sodium chicken broth

1 tablespoon cornstarch

FRITES

1 quart peanut oil

1 pound russet potatoes, peeled and cut
  into even, ⅜-inch-thick strips

Salt

For the roast chicken, preheat the oven to 375°F.

Rinse the inner cavity of the chicken to remove any pooled blood; pat dry. Place the chicken on a rack in a medium-sized, shallow roasting pan. Mash the garlic and salt together with the tines of a fork on a cutting board to form a paste. Stir the butter, thyme, pepper, and mashed garlic together in a small bowl to combine. Using your fingers, rub half of the butter mixture under the skin and over the breast meat of the chicken. Rub the remaining butter mixture over the outer surface of the chicken. Place the onion in the cavity of the chicken. Pour the white wine and ½ cup of the broth into the roasting pan. Roast for 1 hour 20 minutes to 1½ hours or until a thermometer registers 180°F when inserted in the thickest portion of the thigh and the juices run clear. Remove the chicken to a platter. Remove the rack.

Mix 2 tablespoons of water with the cornstarch in a small bowl; set aside. Add the remaining ½ cup of broth to the roasting pan along with ½ cup of water. Scrape the bottom to combine the drippings; tilt the pan and skim off some of the surface fat with a spoon. Bring the liquid to a boil over medium heat. Whisk in the cornstarch mixture; cook until thickened, about 1 minute. Serve with the chicken.

Meanwhile, for the fries, heat the peanut oil to between 350°F and 360°F in a large frying pan. Add the potatoes, in 3 to 4 batches, and fry until just beginning to color, maintaining the oil temperature, 3 to 5 minutes per batch. Drain on paper towels.

When ready to serve, reheat the peanut oil to between 375°F and 380°F. Re-fry the potatoes in 3 to 4 batches until browned and crisp, maintaining the oil temperature, 2 to 3 minutes per batch. Drain; salt and serve immediately.

TRUCS:

PLACING THE CHICKEN ON A RACK ABOVE THE WINE AND BROTH PRODUCES EXCELLENT RESULTS AND ELIMINATES SEVERAL STEPS FROM THE TRADITIONAL FRENCH ROASTING METHOD. ELEVATING THE CHICKEN ALLOWS THE SKIN TO BROWN NICELY WHILE THE STEAM FORMED FROM THE EVAPORATING LIQUID KEEPS THE FLESH MOIST WITHOUT BASTING. THIS ELIMINATES THE NEED TO BROWN THE CHICKEN IN A SKILLET BEFORE ROASTING AND ELIMINATES THE CLASSIC STEP OF TURNING THE CHICKEN FROM SIDE TO SIDE IN THE OVEN TO KEEP THE BREAST MEAT MOIST.

CRISP FRIES CAN BE MADE AT HOME. HAVING NO COMMERCIAL FRYER, I FIND AN ELECTRIC FRYING PAN PRODUCES GOOD RESULTS. DO NOT OVERCROWD THE PAN; IF YOU DO, THE OIL TEMPERATURE FLUCTUATES TOO MUCH AND THE FRIES ABSORB TOO MUCH OIL. DOUBLE FRYING IS AN ABSOLUTE NECESSITY, PRODUCING A FLUFFY INTERIOR AND CRISP EXTERIOR.

CHICKEN WITH CARAMELIZED ONIONS

Roast chicken takes on a whole new character when surrounded by caramelized onions. Naturally sweet, baby onions brown very well into appealingly rich, coffee-colored ovals with only a bit of time and attention.

MAKES 4 SERVINGS

One 16-ounce package frozen baby
  onions, thawed

1⅓ cups reduced-sodium chicken broth

½ cup plus ⅓ cup white wine

3 tablespoons salted butter

2 tablespoons sugar

½ teaspoon dried thyme

1 bay leaf

1½ teaspoons white wine vinegar

One 3½- to 4-pound chicken

1½ teaspoons minced garlic

¼ teaspoon salt

¼ teaspoon freshly ground pepper

Preheat the oven to 375°F.

Combine the baby onions, ⅓ cup of the broth, ⅓ cup of the white wine, 1 tablespoon of the butter, the sugar, ¼ teaspoon of the thyme, and the bay leaf in a large skillet. Heat over medium-high heat; cook until all the liquid has evaporated, stirring occasionally, about 10 minutes. Remove the bay leaf. Continue cooking until the onions brown and caramelize, stirring gently as needed to prevent burning, 6 to 8 minutes. Stir in the white wine vinegar; cook until evaporated, 30 seconds to 1 minute. Set aside in the skillet.

Rinse the inner cavity of the chicken to remove any pooled blood; pat dry. Place the chicken on a rack in a medium-sized, shallow roasting pan. Mash the garlic and salt together with the tines of a fork on a cutting board to form a paste. Stir the remaining 2 tablespoons of butter, the remaining ¼ teaspoon of thyme, the pepper, and the mashed garlic together in a small bowl to combine. Using your fingers, rub half of the butter mixture under the skin and over the breast meat of the chicken. Rub the remaining butter mixture over the outer surface of the chicken. Spoon ½ cup of the caramelized onions into the cavity. Pour the remaining 1 cup of broth and ½ cup of white wine into the roasting pan. Roast for 1 hour 20 minutes to 1½ hours or until a thermometer registers 180°F when inserted in the thickest portion of the thigh and the juices run clear. Remove the chicken to a platter and remove the onions from the cavity; add to the other onions in the skillet. Remove the rack and drain the fat from the roasting pan.

Add 2 tablespoons of water to the skillet and stir to dissolve any caramelized residue on the bottom of the skillet. Add to the roasting pan and heat briefly over medium-low heat until the onions are warmed, adding up to an additional ¼ cup of water or wine if necessary to dissolve and combine any caramelized roasting juices, 2 to 3 minutes. Surround the chicken on the platter with the onions and the pan juices and serve.

✳

TRUC:

THE AMOUNT OF ROASTING JUICES ACCUMULATED ON THE BOTTOM OF THE PAN DEPENDS ON ITS SIZE. TRY TO CHOOSE A SHALLOW, HEAVY PAN ONLY SLIGHTLY LARGER THAN THE CHICKEN. IF THE PAN HAS A LARGE SURFACE AREA, THE ROASTING JUICES MAY HAVE ALL EVAPORATED, LEAVING ONLY A CARAMELIZED RESIDUE THAT REQUIRES EXTRA LIQUID TO LOOSEN.

CHICKEN ROASTED WITH WHISKEY AND SHALLOTS

Cut in pieces and casserole roasted, this lovely chicken rests on the strength of its ingredients. Make sure to use a quality bird and don't skimp on the whiskey, which is what the French call Scotch. If Scotch is not your tipple, Cognac or brandy will work as well.

Napped with a crème fraîche topping, this dish calls for a mound of rice to soak up every last drop of sauce.

MAKES 4 SERVINGS

1 tablespoon salted butter

1 tablespoon canola oil

One 3½- to 4-pound chicken, cut into 8 pieces
  (see Note, page 123)

½ teaspoon salt

⅛ teaspoon freshly ground pepper

⅓ cup Scotch whiskey

1 cup chopped shallots

½ teaspoon dried thyme

1 cup white wine

¼ cup crème fraîche

Preheat the oven to 375°F.

Heat the butter and canola oil in a large skillet over medium-high heat. When sizzling, add the chicken, seasoned with the salt and pepper, in batches. Sauté until well browned on both sides, 4 to 5 minutes per side. Return all the chicken pieces to the skillet; pour the Scotch over the chicken. Immediately light with a match to flame and cook until the flames disappear. Transfer in a single layer to a shallow roasting pan. Sprinkle with the shallots and thyme. Pour the white wine into the skillet; bring to a simmer, scraping up any brown bits from the bottom of the skillet. Pour over the chicken. Roast for 40 to 50 minutes or until the thighs are not pink in the thickest portion when cut with a knife. Remove to a platter; cover with aluminum foil to keep warm.

Heat the roasting pan over medium-high heat; whisk in the crème fraîche. Boil until thickened slightly and reduced, 2 to 3 minutes. Spoon over the chicken and serve.

TRUC:
MAKING CRÈME FRAÎCHE AT HOME IS EASY. HEAT 1 CUP OF HEAVY CREAM UNTIL IT IS JUST BARELY LUKEWARM, ABOUT BABY-BOTTLE TEMPERATURE. STIR IN 2 TABLESPOONS OF BUTTERMILK—MOST RECIPES CALL FOR 1 TABLESPOON BUT I FIND 2 WORK BETTER. LET THE CREAM MIXTURE SIT IN A BOWL AT ROOM TEMPERATURE, COVERED, UNTIL THICKENED, ABOUT 24 HOURS. REFRIGERATE, COVERED, UNTIL READY TO USE. THE CRÈME FRAÎCHE WILL CONTINUE TO THICKEN SLIGHTLY IN THE REFRIGERATOR.

ROCK CORNISH GAME HENS
WITH MUSTARD

The mustard–crème fraîche coating keeps everything well basted and succulent during roasting. You'll find these little birds equally delightful packed in a picnic hamper and served at room temperature, with the sauce served on the side for dipping. Cornish game hens are more readily available than true poussins; either will work. For the adventuresome cook, I suggest trying this recipe using a cut-up rabbit.

MAKES 6 SERVINGS

1 tablespoon canola oil

3 Rock Cornish game hens or 3 poussins,
   split in half lengthwise

½ teaspoon salt

¼ teaspoon freshly ground pepper

⅓ cup tarragon-Dijon mustard

⅓ cup Dijon mustard

⅓ cup crème fraîche

½ cup reduced-sodium chicken broth

1 tablespoon red wine vinegar

1 tablespoon cornstarch

Preheat the oven to 375°F.

Heat the canola oil in a large skillet over medium-high heat. Add the hens, skin side down, seasoned with the salt and pepper, in batches; sauté until well browned, 4 to 5 minutes. Remove to a shallow roasting or baking pan. Combine both mustards and the crème fraîche. Brush both sides of the hens with about half the mustard mixture and arrange in a single layer, skin side up. Add the broth to the skillet; bring to a simmer, scraping up any brown bits from the bottom of the skillet. Whisk in the remaining mustard mixture and pour into the bottom of the roasting pan. Bake for 45 minutes or until the juices run clear in the portion between the thigh and the leg when cut with a knife. Remove to a serving platter; cover with aluminum foil to keep warm.

Combine the red wine vinegar and cornstarch. Heat the sauce in the roasting pan on medium-low heat; bring to a simmer. Whisk in the cornstarch mixture and simmer briefly to thicken slightly, 1 to 2 minutes. Serve with the game hens.

TRUC:

HAVE YOUR BUTCHER SPLIT THE BIRDS FOR YOU. THIS IS SOMETHING THEY CAN EASILY DO EVEN IF THE BIRDS ARE FROZEN.

SUPRÊMES DE VOLAILLE À LA DIABLE

DEVILED CHICKEN BREASTS

The term à la diable, or deviled, refers to the spiciness of the coating. Most likely borrowed from the English, the technique lends itself particularly well to intense French mustard. While sometimes completed with a layer of bread crumbs and served with a spicy sauce, this version packs in plenty of zip with little effort.

MAKES 4 SERVINGS

½ teaspoon salt

½ teaspoon dried thyme

¼ teaspoon freshly ground pepper

4 bone-in, skin-on chicken breasts

1 tablespoon plus 1 teaspoon olive oil

2 tablespoons Dijon mustard

1½ teaspoons fresh lemon juice

½ teaspoon dry mustard

Pinch cayenne

Place an oven rack about 6 inches from the broiler element. Heat the broiler. Mix together the salt, thyme, and pepper; sprinkle over both sides of the breasts. Drizzle both sides with the 1 tablespoon of olive oil; rub to coat all surfaces. Place on a broiler pan. Broil skin side up for 6 to 8 minutes, until well browned; turn and broil for an additional 8 minutes. Mix the Dijon mustard, lemon juice, dry mustard, cayenne, and the remaining 1 teaspoon of olive oil in a small bowl. Remove the breasts from the broiler; turn off the broiler and set the oven temperature at 450°F. Turn the breasts skin side up; spoon the mustard mixture over the breasts and spread to coat. Bake for 10 minutes or until the chicken is no longer pink in the thickest portion when cut with a knife.

✳

TRUC:

SOME STORES CARRY MOUTARDE EXTRA-FORTE (EXTRA-HOT); IF IT'S AVAILABLE USE IT AS A SUBSTITUTE FOR THE DIJON MUSTARD AND OMIT THE DRY MUSTARD. THE MAILLE BRAND MARKETS THIS ESPECIALLY PIQUANT CONDIMENT IN SOME UPSCALE STORES IN THIS COUNTRY.

CHICKEN BREASTS WITH HONEY, LAVENDER, AND HERBS

Throughout the hillsides of Provence, especially in the département called the Drôme, lavender grows in purple swatches, popping into vision between green valleys to emulate a patchwork quilt. Mostly used in beauty products and cleaning aids—washing the floor with lavender water keeps the scorpions away—it also appears as a seasoning. These quick-roasted breasts perfume the house with sweet-savory aromas as they cook to a succulent crispness.

MAKES 4 SERVINGS

1 tablespoon lavender honey if available or honey

1 tablespoon fresh lemon juice

1 tablespoon salted butter, melted

1 teaspoon herbes de Provence with lavender

1 teaspoon dried lavender flowers

¼ teaspoon salt

⅛ teaspoon freshly ground pepper

4 bone-in, skin-on chicken breasts

¼ cup white wine

Preheat the oven to 425°F.

Stir together the honey, lemon juice, butter, herbes de Provence, lavender, salt, and pepper in a small bowl. Arrange the breasts, skin side up, in a single layer in a shallow roasting pan. Spoon the honey mixture evenly over the breasts; rub over all. Roast for 25 to 30 minutes or until the breasts are no longer pink in the thickest portion when cut with a knife. Remove to a platter.

Add the white wine to the roasting pan; heat over medium-high heat until boiling, scraping up all the darkly caramelized bits on the bottom of the pan, 1 to 2 minutes. Spoon over the chicken and serve.

TRUC:

HERBES DE PROVENCE ARE A BLEND OF
SEASONINGS INCLUDING THYME, ROSEMARY,
BASIL, SAVORY, MARJORAM, AND, SOMETIMES,
LAVENDER. IN POINT OF FACT, MOST OF THE
BLENDS SOLD IN PROVENCE DON'T CONTAIN
ANY LAVENDER, WHILE MOST OF THE BLENDS
SOLD IN THIS COUNTRY DO. IF THE TYPE YOU
PURCHASE IS WITHOUT, ADD AN EXTRA PINCH
OF DRIED LAVENDER FLOWERS WHEN
PREPARING THIS RECIPE. WHEN BUYING
LAVENDER IN FARMERS' MARKETS HERE,
MAKE SURE IT'S NOT BEEN TREATED WITH
CHEMICALS AND IS SAFE TO EAT. IT CAN
ALSO BE MAIL-ORDERED.

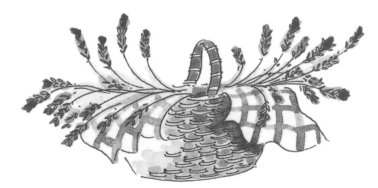

TAGINE DE POULET

CHICKEN TAGINE

With a significant minority of the French population being of North African origin, dishes like tagines are part of the culinary landscape throughout France.

A tagine is a Moroccan conical earthenware cooking pot used to make slow-cooking stews over a small charcoal heat source. The stews themselves carry the name of the utensil. The term tagine calls up images of braised meat and/or vegetables in a concentrated sauce reduced through evaporation during cooking.

MAKES 4 SERVINGS

One 3½- to 4-pound chicken, cut into 8 pieces
(see Note, page 123) or 8 skinless, bone-in
chicken thighs
1 medium onion, finely chopped
3 garlic cloves, minced
¾ teaspoon ground ginger
½ teaspoon salt
¼ teaspoon freshly ground pepper
¼ teaspoon turmeric
Pinch cayenne
⅛ teaspoon saffron threads, crushed
1 tablespoon extra virgin olive oil
1 pound package baby carrots
¼ cup fresh lemon juice
¾ cup pitted kalamata olives
2 tablespoons chopped fresh cilantro

Preheat the oven to 325°F.

Place the chicken pieces in the bottom of a large Dutch oven with the breasts layered on top of the thighs and drumsticks. Scatter the onion and garlic over the chicken. Mix the ginger, salt, pepper, turmeric, and cayenne together in a small bowl; sprinkle over the chicken. Stir the saffron into 1 cup of hot water; pour over all. Drizzle with the olive oil. Cover the chicken, leaving the lid slightly ajar. Bake for 1½ hours; add the carrots and lemon juice. Bake with the cover slightly ajar for an additional 30 minutes, until the carrots are tender. Add the olives; sprinkle with the cilantro and serve.

TRUCS:

IN CONTEMPORARY KITCHENS, EARTHENWARE TAGINES ARE BEST USED IN AN OVEN BUT THEY AREN'T NECESSARY TO PRODUCE EXCELLENT RESULTS. USE A HEAVY DUTCH OVEN INSTEAD. LEAVING THE COVER AJAR DURING COOKING ALLOWS SOME OF THE MOISTURE TO ESCAPE AND INTENSIFIES THE ESSENCE OF THE SAUCE.

MANY TAGINE RECIPES CALL FOR ADDITIONAL OLIVE OIL, BUT CONTEMPORARY TASTE IS FOR LESS ACCUMULATED FAT AND OIL ON THE SURFACE OF SAUCES. USING SKINLESS CHICKEN THIGHS IS ANOTHER WAY TO REDUCE THE TOTAL AMOUNT OF FAT IN THE FINAL DISH WITHOUT SACRIFICING MOIST AND TENDER MEAT.

PROVENÇAL TIAN WITH CHICKEN

Once again, the container lends its name to the food. Like a terrine or tagine, a tian is a cooking vessel, in this case, a shallow pottery baking dish most often used to cook vegetables. Adding chicken to the layers, a trick suggested by my friend Christiane Deuwille at the Hôtel St. Marc in our village, turns an accompaniment into a robust main course.

MAKES 4 SERVINGS

4 tablespoons olive oil

2 medium or 1 large eggplant (about 1¼ pounds total), sliced ½ inch thick

1 large onion, sliced ⅛ inch thick

1 tablespoon minced garlic

¾ teaspoon salt

½ teaspoon dried thyme

¼ teaspoon dried oregano

¼ teaspoon freshly ground pepper

Four 5-ounce boneless, skinless chicken breasts

½ cup lightly packed fresh basil leaves

3 large Roma tomatoes (about ½ pound), sliced ⅛ inch thick

2 small zucchini (scant ½ pound), quarter-sized in diameter, sliced ⅛ inch thick

Preheat the oven to 375°F. Oil the bottom and sides of a 2½- to 3-quart oval glass or pottery baking dish with 1 tablespoon of the olive oil.

Cook the eggplant in a large pot of salted, boiling water until tender, 5 to 7 minutes; drain well. When cool enough to handle, lay the slices flat on several layers of paper towels; gently press with additional paper towels to dry as much as possible.

Heat 1 tablespoon of the olive oil in a large skillet over medium-high heat. Add the onion; sauté until softened and just beginning to brown, 4 to 5 minutes. Spread in the bottom of the prepared pan. Arrange the eggplant slices in a single layer over the onion. Sprinkle with half of the garlic. Combine the salt, thyme, oregano, and pepper; sprinkle the eggplant with a third of the salt-herb mixture.

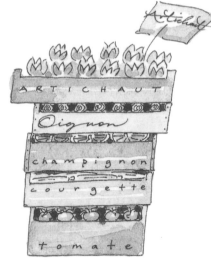

TRUC:

THE EGGPLANT NEEDS TO BE PRECOOKED BEFORE BEING ADDED TO THE TIAN. FRYING USES TOO MUCH OIL. BOILING THE EGGPLANT INSTEAD OF BAKING IT IS A QUICK-COOKING SOLUTION, TAKING ONLY ABOUT 5 MINUTES INSTEAD OF THE 30 TO 40 MINUTES EGGPLANT NEEDS IN THE OVEN TO TENDERIZE.

Cut the breasts in half crosswise; flatten with a mallet or top with plastic wrap and flatten with a rolling pin to a scant ½-inch thickness. Arrange the breast pieces in a single layer over the eggplant; season with the remaining garlic and another third of the herb-salt mixture. Scatter the basil leaves over all. Arrange the tomato slices and zucchini slices in alternating, overlapping rows over all; season with the remaining third of the herb-salt mixture and drizzle with the remaining 2 tablespoons of olive oil. Bake for 50 to 60 minutes, until the chicken is no longer pink when cut with a knife.

TOURTIÈRE DE POULET

Chicken Pot Pie with Puff Pastry

We call them pot pies; the French call them tourtières *and top them with multilayered puff pastry for a decadent touch. Salsify, a root vegetable, is often used in this dish but can be tricky to find. Parsnips work equally well and add a pleasant, sweet-nutty starchiness to the finished pie.*

MAKES 6 SERVINGS

1 tablespoon canola oil

1 tablespoon salted butter

6 boneless, skinless chicken thighs

¼ teaspoon salt

⅛ teaspoon freshly ground pepper

½ cup chopped shallots

2 tablespoons all-purpose flour

¾ cup white wine

½ teaspoon dried thyme

1 bay leaf

½ pound white button mushrooms, quartered

2 medium parsnips, peeled and cut into
   1½ × ½ × ½-inch strips

1 medium carrot, peeled and cut into
   1½ × ½ × ½-inch strips

1 tablespoon lemon juice

One-half 17.3-ounce box frozen puff pastry
   (1 sheet), thawed

Heat the canola oil and butter in a Dutch oven over medium-high heat. When sizzling, add the chicken thighs, seasoned with the salt and pepper; sauté until well browned on both sides, 4 to 5 minutes per side. Remove. Add the shallots; sauté until softened, 3 to 4 minutes. Sprinkle with flour; cook, stirring often, to remove the floury taste, about 1 minute. Return the thighs to the Dutch oven; add the white wine, ¾ cup of water, the thyme, and the bay leaf. Reduce the heat to low; cover and cook for 15 minutes. Add the mushrooms, parsnips, carrot, and lemon juice; stir gently to combine. Cover and cook until the vegetables are tender, about 30 minutes. Remove the chicken thighs; let cool. Remove the vegetables with a slotted spoon to a 9-inch deep-dish glass pie pan or 9-inch round baking dish; let cool. Increase the heat to high; boil the sauce in the Dutch oven until reduced to 1 cup, 4 to 5 minutes; remove the bay leaf.

Preheat the oven to 400°F.

When the chicken is cool, cut into chunks. Stir into the sauce; spoon into the pie pan. Dust a countertop lightly with flour; roll out the sheet of puff pastry to a 10-inch square. Cut into a 10-inch circle and center on top of the pie pan, easing the overhang gently into the plate and pressing the cut edges firmly against the sides of the pie pan. Cut a vent in the center of the pastry. Bake for 15 minutes, until the top is browned and the filling is heated through. Serve.

TRUC:

MAKE SURE TO CUT THE PUFF PASTRY CIRCLE LARGER THAN THE DIAMETER OF THE BAKING PAN. THE PUFF PASTRY WILL CONTRACT SLIGHTLY WHEN LIFTED FROM THE COUNTERTOP AND EVEN MORE IN BAKING.

Poulets aux Pots

Braises and Stews

CHICKEN WING STEW

Alicot *(or alicuit, alycot, or alycou)* is a derivation of aile et cou *(wing and neck)* in dialect. This dish is yet another French way to turn almost everything, excluding the cackle, into a savory meal. Besides chicken, duck, or goose wings, necks and gizzards are often used. It is traditional to the Béarn area of France, located well below Bordeaux and next to the Pyrénées, but common throughout the southwest, providing an economically delectable dinner. Serve it with mashed potatoes or noodles.

MAKES 4 SERVINGS

2 to 2½ pounds chicken wings or a combination
  of chicken wings and gizzards

1 tablespoon olive oil

2 medium onions, chopped

3 large garlic cloves

1 tablespoon all-purpose flour

One 14-ounce can reduced-sodium chicken broth

3 large carrots, chopped

One 14½-ounce can diced tomatoes, drained

1 bay leaf

¼ teaspoon dried thyme

⅛ teaspoon crumbled dried rosemary

⅛ teaspoon freshly ground pepper

Trim the tips from the wings; pat dry. (Reserve the tips in the freezer for later use in making broths or stock.) Heat the olive oil in a large skillet over medium-high heat. When hot, add the wings in batches; sauté until well browned on both sides, 3 to 4 minutes per side. Remove to a Dutch oven. Put the onions in the skillet; reduce the heat to medium. Sauté until browned, 4 to 6 minutes. Add the garlic; sauté until fragrant, 30 seconds to 1 minute. Sprinkle with the flour; stir to blend well. Slowly whisk in the broth, scraping up any brown bits from the bottom of the skillet. Pour into the Dutch oven; add the carrots, tomatoes, and bay leaf. Sprinkle with the thyme, rosemary, and pepper; stir to combine. Bring just to a boil over medium heat, 5 to 8 minutes; reduce the heat to low. Simmer with the cover slightly ajar until fork tender, stirring occasionally, 1 to 1½ hours. Remove the bay leaf before serving.

✳

TRUC:

GARLIC BURNS VERY EASILY, SO ADD IT AFTER THE ONIONS ARE BROWNED. THAT WAY, IT SAUTÉS BRIEFLY. WHEN THE AROMA FILLS THE KITCHEN, IT'S TIME TO ADD SOME LIQUID TO KEEP THE GARLIC FROM BURNING.

BOUILLABAISSE DE POULET

Chicken Bouillabaisse

When the weather turns colder, the posted menus in our northern part of Provence change from lighter fare to warming stews. Since the Mediterranean is more than a stone's throw away, offering chicken bouillabaisse instead of fish is an economical compromise between Provençal tradition and easily procured ingredients.

MAKES 6 SERVINGS

1 tablespoon olive oil

6 bone-in, skin-on chicken thighs

6 bone-in, skin-on chicken drumsticks

2 medium fennel bulbs, cut into 1-inch chunks

1 large onion, cut into ½-inch wedges

1 tablespoon minced garlic

1 cup white wine

½ teaspoon saffron threads, crumbled

One 28-ounce can diced tomatoes in juice

1 cup reduced-sodium chicken broth

¼ teaspoon freshly ground pepper

2 tablespoons Pernod

2 tablespoons chopped fresh parsley

1 tablespoon chopped fresh basil

Croutons (croutes; see Note)

ROUILLE

3 large garlic cloves

½ teaspoon salt

¾ cup good-quality mayonnaise

⅓ cup extra virgin olive oil

½ teaspoon saffron threads, crumbled

¼ teaspoon cayenne

Heat the olive oil in a large skillet over medium-high heat. When hot, add the chicken in batches, and sauté until golden brown on both sides, 3 to 4 minutes per side. Remove to a Dutch oven. Add the fennel and onion; sauté until beginning to soften, 4 to 5 minutes. Add the garlic; sauté until fragrant, 30 seconds to 1 minute. Remove to the Dutch oven. Add the white wine to the skillet; bring to a simmer, scraping up any brown bits from the bottom of the skillet. Add the saffron; stir to dissolve. Pour into the Dutch oven; add the tomatoes, broth, and pepper. Bring just to a boil over medium heat, 7 to 10 minutes; reduce the heat to low. Simmer with the cover just slightly ajar until the chicken is tender and the thighs are no longer pink in the thickest portion when cut with a knife, about 1 hour. Stir in the Pernod. Garnish with the parsley and basil. Serve ladled into shallow bowls with the rouille and croutons on the side.

For the rouille, mash the garlic and salt together with the tines of a fork on a cutting board to form a paste; scrape into a food processor. Add the mayonnaise; process while adding the olive oil in a thin stream. Add the saffron and cayenne; process to combine. Refrigerate, covered, until ready to serve.

Note: To make the croutons, slice stale French bread in ½-inch-thick slices. Arrange in a single layer on a shallow baking sheet; brush lightly with olive oil. Rub the surface of one side with a crushed garlic clove. Toast in a 400°F oven for 6 to 8 minutes, until crisp.

TRUCS:

TRADITIONAL ROUILLE IS MADE WITH A RAW EGG YOLK AND OLIVE OIL, IN MUCH THE SAME WAY AS HOMEMADE MAYONNAISE. BECAUSE OF FOOD SAFETY CONCERNS OVER SALMONELLA, I LIKE TO USE COMMERCIALLY PREPARED MAYONNAISE AS A BASE AND ADD OLIVE OIL FOR A MORE AUTHENTIC TASTE.

MASHING THE GARLIC CLOVES WITH SALT BEFORE INCORPORATING THEM REMOVES SOME OF THE RAW GARLIC'S HARSHNESS.

CHICKEN COUSCOUS

*B*ack *in the late '60s, while studying in Paris, I discovered North African food. In the Latin Quarter, lining the twisting, narrow roads that date back to the Middle Ages, were countless Moroccan, Algerian, and Tunisian restaurants and pastry shops. They offered cheap and appetizing food that we students loved. I'd never seen couscous before but it quickly became a favorite, spiked with harissa at the end for extra emphasis.*

MAKES 6 SERVINGS

One 4½- to 5-pound chicken, cut into 8 pieces (see Note, page 123)

One 14½-ounce can diced tomatoes in juice

1 medium onion, cut into 1-inch wedges

2 cinnamon sticks

1 tablespoon olive oil

1 teaspoon salt

½ teaspoon coarsely ground pepper

½ teaspoon ground ginger

2 small turnips, peeled and cut into 1-inch wedges

1 small sweet potato, cut into 1-inch pieces

¾ cup raisins

½ cup baby carrots

1 red or green jalapeño, seeds and membranes removed if desired, minced

One 15-ounce can garbanzo beans, drained and rinsed

1 small zucchini, halved lengthwise and cut into 1½-inch pieces

One 5.4-ounce box couscous

Harissa, optional (see Truc)

Place the chicken in a large Dutch oven; add 4 cups of water, the diced tomatoes with their juice, onion, cinnamon sticks, olive oil, salt, and pepper. Bring just to a boil over medium heat. Reduce the heat to low; simmer for 30 minutes. Sprinkle with the ground ginger; add the turnips, sweet potato, raisins, carrots, and jalapeño. Increase the heat to medium-low; bring back to a simmer. Reduce the heat to low; cook until the vegetables are tender, 30 to 35 minutes. About 15 minutes before serving, add the garbanzo beans and zucchini to the pot; adjust the heat to maintain a gentle simmer. Remove the cinnamon sticks before serving.

Prepare the couscous according to the package directions. Serve the chicken, vegetables, and broth with the couscous. If desired, serve the harissa in a small bowl and provide separate small bowls for each person. If spooned in small amounts into the bowls and diluted with a bit of the broth, the harissa may be spooned over individual portions as desired, with extra heat added to taste.

✳

TRUCS:

COUSCOUS IS REALLY PASTA, MADE FROM SEMOLINA. ALTHOUGH AUTHENTIC COUSCOUS REQUIRES STEAMING IN THE UPPER PERFORATED PORTION OF A POT CALLED A *COUSCOUSSIÈRE* WHILE THE STEW SIMMERS BELOW, THE COUSCOUS FOUND IN SUPERMARKETS IS MUCH QUICKER AND EASIER TO USE.

HARISSA, A TUNISIAN CHILE PEPPER–BASED SAUCE, CAN BE FOUND IN ETHNIC MARKETS AND UPSCALE STORES. LOOK FOR IT IN SMALL CANS, JARS, OR TUBES.

COLOMBO CHICKEN

Although the French often use prepared curry powder to add interest to recipes, this dish puts together its own seasoning powder called poudre de colombo, *a Caribbean term for curry. While visiting the exotic island of Martinique, as much a part of France as Paris, I discovered that the tradition of dining well had safely crossed the Atlantic. This recipe exemplifies a cuisine as impressive as the tropical landscape. Try serving this dish with basmati rice.*

MAKES 6 SERVINGS

POUDRE DE COLOMBO
1½ teaspoons ground coriander
1 teaspoon ground ginger
1 teaspoon dry mustard
½ teaspoon crushed fennel seeds
¼ teaspoon turmeric

One-half 1-pound eggplant, peeled and cut into
   1-inch cubes (about 2 cups)
1½ cups peeled and cubed butternut squash
   (about 1-inch cubes)
1 chayote squash, peeled, seeded, quartered, and
   sliced into 1-inch slices
1 unripened mango, peeled, seeded, and cut into
   ¾-inch dice

2 tablespoons canola oil
3 bone-in, skin-on chicken breasts
3 bone-in, skin-on chicken thighs
3 bone-in, skin-on chicken drumsticks
½ teaspoon salt
¼ teaspoon freshly ground pepper
1 large onion, chopped (about 1½ cups)
3 serrano chiles, seeded and membranes removed
   if desired, finely chopped
1 tablespoon minced garlic
One 14-ounce can reduced-sodium chicken broth
2 teaspoons tamarind concentrate
One 14-ounce can unsweetened coconut milk
1 tablespoon lime juice

For the poudre de colombo, blend the coriander, ginger, mustard, fennel, and turmeric together; set aside.

Place the eggplant, butternut squash, chayote squash, and mango in a Dutch oven.

Heat the canola oil in a large skillet over medium-high heat. Add the chicken, seasoned with the salt and pepper, in batches; sauté until golden brown on both sides, 3 to 4 minutes per side. Remove to the Dutch oven. Add the onion; reduce the heat to medium and sauté until tender, 4 to 5 minutes. Add the serranos, garlic, and poudre de colombo; sauté until fragrant, 30 seconds to 1 minute. Stir in the broth; bring to a simmer, scraping up any brown bits on the bottom of the skillet, 1 to 2 minutes. Whisk in the tamarind. Pour the mixture into the Dutch oven along with the coconut milk. Bring just to a boil over medium heat; reduce the heat to low. Simmer with the cover just partially ajar until the vegetables are tender and the thighs are no longer pink in the thickest portion when cut with a knife, 50 to 60 minutes. Remove the chicken and vegetables to a large shallow bowl such as a pasta bowl; cover with aluminum foil to keep warm.

Bring the cooking liquid to a boil over high heat; cook until reduced by half and slightly thickened, 6 to 8 minutes. Stir in the lime juice; pour over the chicken and serve.

TRUCS:

DIFFERENT PARTS OF THE COUNTRY PACKAGE MEAT IN DIFFERENT WAYS. HERE IN THE MIDWEST, CHICKEN IS SOMETIMES OFFERED IN A PACKAGE CONTAINING 3 BREASTS, 3 THIGHS, AND 3 LEGS. THIS IS A GREAT WAY TO GET THE MEATIEST PORTIONS OF THE BIRD AND ENOUGH CHICKEN TO FEED SIX PEOPLE.

FENNEL SEEDS CAN BE CRUSHED IN A MORTAR AND PESTLE OR SIMPLY FINELY CHOPPED WITH THE BLADE OF A KNIFE.

LEAVING THE SEEDS AND MEMBRANES IN THE SERRANO CHILES SUBSTANTIALLY INCREASES THE SPICY HEAT THEY CONTRIBUTE TO THIS DISH.

TAMARIND IS USED IN MANY WARM-WEATHER CUISINES. IT HAS A TANGY FLAVOR THAT WORKS WELL WITH SPICED FOODS. LOOK FOR IT IN HISPANIC OR INDIAN ETHNIC MARKETS; IF UNAVAILABLE, SUBSTITUTE RED WINE VINEGAR.

COQ À LA BIÈRE
CHICKEN WITH ALE

North of Paris, around industrial Lille, beer becomes an important beverage, gaining influence from nearby Belgium. Instead of wine, chicken cozies up with ale and the two snugly simmer together to the benefit of both the stew and the diner.

MAKES 4 SERVINGS

2 tablespoons canola oil

One 3½- to 4-pound cut-up chicken

¼ teaspoon salt

⅛ teaspoon freshly ground pepper

4 juniper berries, crushed and chopped

½ teaspoon cumin seeds

2 medium onions, sliced

1 teaspoon light brown sugar

1½ cups French country ale or Alsatian beer

One 14-ounce can reduced-sodium chicken broth

1 bouquet garni (2 sprigs parsley, 2 sprigs thyme, and 1 bay leaf, tied together with twine)

2 tablespoons cornstarch

Heat the canola oil in a large skillet over medium-high heat. Add the chicken, seasoned with the salt and pepper, skin side down. Sauté until well browned, 4 to 5 minutes. Turn and sauté until well browned, 4 to 5 minutes. Remove to a Dutch oven. Add the juniper berries and cumin seeds; toast for a few seconds, then stir in the onions. Reduce the heat to medium; sauté until softened, 4 to 5 minutes. Sprinkle with the sugar; continue cooking until beginning to brown, 3 to 4 minutes. Add 1¼ cups of the beer; bring to a simmer, scraping up any brown bits from the bottom of the skillet, 2 to 3 minutes. Pour into the Dutch oven along with the broth and bouquet garni. Bring just to a boil over medium heat, 4 to 7 minutes; reduce the heat to low. Simmer with the cover just slightly ajar until the thighs are no longer pink in the thickest portion when cut with a knife, 45 to 60 minutes. Remove the chicken; cover with aluminum foil to keep warm. Discard the bouquet garni.

Increase the heat to high and boil until reduced by half, 8 to 10 minutes. Taste and adjust the seasonings. Combine the cornstarch with the remaining ¼ cup of beer; whisk into the boiling sauce. Boil until thickened, 1 to 2 minutes. Reduce the heat to medium-low; return the chicken to the Dutch oven and simmer briefly to rewarm, 1 to 2 minutes. Serve.

TRUCS:

IN THE PAST, CHICKEN STEW USED OLD, TOUGH ROOSTERS *(COQS)* OR HENS AND REQUIRED LONG, GENTLE COOKING TO TENDERIZE THE MEAT. TODAY'S MARKETS STOCK MUCH YOUNGER BIRDS THAT REQUIRE MUCH LESS COOKING TIME.

TO MAKE USING A BOUQUET GARNI TRULY EFFORTLESS, LOOK FOR A GIANT TEA BALL AT AN UPSCALE COOKWARE STORE. PUT THE PARSLEY, THYME, AND BAY LEAF IN THE MESH BALL AND SKIP SEARCHING FOR THE KITCHEN TWINE AND TYING EVERYTHING TOGETHER.

CHICKEN WITH RIESLING

When in Alsace, do as the Alsatians do; that is, make a successful variation on coq au vin using the local Riesling wine. Plump pieces of poultry, mushrooms, and straw-colored wine simmered together and laced with cream prove that chicken stew can be made in many delicious ways.

MAKES 6 SERVINGS

One 3½- to 4-pound cut-up chicken

2 bone-in, skin-on chicken breasts

1 tablespoon canola oil

1 tablespoon salted butter

½ teaspoon salt

¼ teaspoon freshly ground pepper

⅔ cup chopped shallots

8 ounces white button mushrooms, quartered

3 cups dry French Alsatian Riesling

1 cup reduced-sodium chicken broth

½ teaspoon dried thyme

½ cup heavy cream

2 tablespoons all-purpose flour

1 tablespoon fresh lemon juice

Cut all the breasts in half crosswise across the bone. Heat the canola oil and butter in a large skillet over medium-high heat. When sizzling, sauté the chicken, seasoned with the salt and pepper, in batches, until golden brown on both sides, 3 to 4 minutes per side. Remove to a large Dutch oven, arranging the breast meat on top of the thighs and drumsticks. Add the shallots to the skillet; sauté until tender, 3 to 4 minutes. Add to the Dutch oven along with the mushrooms and Riesling. Add the broth to the skillet; bring to a simmer, scraping up any brown bits from the bottom of the skillet, 1 to 2 minutes. Stir in the thyme; pour into the Dutch oven. Bring just to a boil over medium heat. Reduce the heat to low and simmer with the cover just partially ajar until the chicken is tender and the thighs are no longer pink in the thickest portion when cut with a knife, 45 to 60 minutes. Remove the chicken; cover with aluminum foil to keep warm.

Increase the heat to high and boil the liquid until reduced by half, about 10 minutes; add the cream. Whisk the flour with 3 tablespoons of water in a small bowl; slowly whisk into the liquid. Boil until slightly thickened, 2 to 3 minutes. Stir in the lemon juice. Reduce the heat to medium-low; return the chicken to the Dutch oven and simmer briefly to rewarm, 1 to 2 minutes.

✳

TRUCS:
TO KEEP THE HALVED CHICKEN BREAST PIECES FROM DRYING OUT DURING COOKING, ARRANGE THEM ON TOP OF THE THIGHS AND DRUMSTICKS IN THE DUTCH OVEN. BREAST MEAT NORMALLY TAKES LESS TIME THAN THIGH MEAT TO COOK; BY PLACING THE BREAST PIECES SLIGHTLY FURTHER FROM THE HEAT SOURCE, YOU EVEN THE COOKING TIME.

IF YOU'RE FEELING PARTICULARLY INDULGENT, MAKE THE COQ AU RIESLING USING 8 OUNCES OF SLICED CHANTERELLE MUSHROOMS INSTEAD OF THE WHITE BUTTON VARIETY. SAUTÉ THEM WITH THE SHALLOTS UNTIL BEGINNING TO SOFTEN, ABOUT 5 MINUTES.

COQ AU VIN
CHICKEN IN RED WINE

The quintessential French chicken stew, coq au vin needs only crusty French bread and a few boiled potatoes to mop up its abundant juices.

MAKES 6 SERVINGS

2 tablespoons canola oil

4 ounces salt pork, diced

8 ounces white button mushrooms, cleaned
  and quartered

1 cup frozen baby onions, thawed

3 bone-in, skin-on chicken breasts

3 bone-in, skin-on chicken thighs

3 bone-in, skin-on chicken drumsticks

¼ teaspoon salt

⅛ teaspoon freshly ground pepper

¼ cup Cognac

One 14-ounce can reduced-sodium chicken broth

3 large garlic cloves, minced

1 bouquet garni (2 sprigs parsley, 2 sprigs
  thyme, and 1 bay leaf, tied together with twine)

1 tablespoon tomato paste

1 bottle red Burgundy wine or Pinot Noir

3 tablespoons all-purpose flour

Heat 1 tablespoon of the canola oil in a large skillet over medium-high heat. When hot, add the salt pork; sauté until crisp, 3 to 4 minutes. Remove with a slotted spoon to a Dutch oven. Add the mushrooms and onions to the skillet; sauté until lightly browned, 5 to 6 minutes. Remove to the Dutch oven. Add the remaining 1 tablespoon of canola oil. When hot, add the chicken, seasoned with the salt and pepper, in batches; sauté until very well browned on both sides, 5 to 6 minutes per side. Remove the chicken. Pour off any fat from the skillet. Return the chicken to the skillet; pour the Cognac over the chicken. Immediately light with a match to flame and cook until the flames disappear. Add the chicken and any pan juices to the Dutch oven. Add the broth to the skillet; bring to a simmer, scraping up any brown bits from the bottom of the skillet. Pour into the Dutch oven; add the garlic, bouquet garni, and tomato paste. Pour in the red wine. Bring just to a boil over medium heat; reduce the heat to low. Simmer with the cover just slightly ajar until the chicken is tender and the thighs are no longer pink in the thickest portion when cut with a knife, 50 to 60 minutes. Remove the chicken; cover with aluminum foil to keep warm. Discard the bouquet garni.

Increase the heat to high and bring the liquid to a boil. Boil until reduced to about 4 cups, 8 to 10 minutes. Whisk the flour with 3 tablespoons of water in a small bowl; slowly whisk into the liquid. Boil until slightly thickened, 1 to 2 minutes. Reduce the heat to medium-low; return the chicken to the Dutch oven and simmer briefly to rewarm, 1 to 2 minutes. Serve.

TRUC:

THE COQ, OR CHICKEN, IN COQ AU VIN NEEDS THOROUGH BROWNING FOR OPTIMUM TASTE AND APPEARANCE. THE BROWNER THE CHICKEN BEFORE ITS RED WINE BATH, THE RICHER THE FINAL COLOR, SUBDUING THE GRAPEY TINT OF THE WINE.

Chicken Thigh Fricassee with Porcini Mushrooms and Tarragon

Every market and every restaurant throughout Provence seems to have its own cèpe festival during the autumn months. Looking like a Disneyesque version of what a mushroom should be, with sturdy stems and generous caps, these members of the bolete family, called porcini in Italy, make their way into the humblest of dishes. Because fresh cèpes are often difficult to find in American markets, dried porcini, with their concentrated essence, stand in for the fresh version here.

MAKES 6 SERVINGS

1 ounce dried porcini mushrooms (cèpes)

2 tablespoons canola oil

1 tablespoon salted butter

¾ cup chopped shallots

1 pound white button mushrooms, quartered

1 cup reduced-sodium chicken broth

6 bone-in, skin-on chicken thighs

6 bone-in, skin-on chicken drumsticks

¼ teaspoon salt

¼ teaspoon freshly ground pepper

1½ cups white wine

1 teaspoon dried tarragon

½ cup heavy cream

Soak the porcini mushrooms in a small bowl with 1 cup of hot water for 30 minutes. Remove the mushrooms with a slotted spoon; coarsely chop. Strain the soaking liquid through a coffee filter or a paper towel in a small strainer.

Heat 1 tablespoon of the canola oil and the butter in a large skillet over medium heat. When sizzling, add the shallots and sauté until softened and just beginning to brown, 4 to 5 minutes. Add the button mushrooms; sauté until beginning to soften, 5 to 8 minutes. Add the porcini mushrooms and the strained soaking liquid. Cook until all the liquid is absorbed, 4 to 5 minutes. Add to a Dutch oven along with the broth.

Heat the remaining 1 tablespoon of canola oil in the same skillet over medium heat. When hot, add the chicken thighs and drumsticks, seasoned with the salt and pepper, in batches; sauté until well browned, 4 to 5 minutes per side. Remove to the Dutch oven. Pour off any fat from the skillet. Add the white wine to the skillet; bring to a simmer, scraping up any brown bits from the bottom of the skillet, 2 to 3 minutes. Add ½ teaspoon of the tarragon; pour into the Dutch oven. Bring just to a boil over medium heat; reduce the heat to low. Simmer with the cover just slightly ajar until the thighs and drumsticks are fork tender, 1 to 1¼ hours. Remove the chicken and mushrooms with a slotted spoon; cover with aluminum foil to keep warm.

Increase the heat to high; add the cream and boil until reduced to 2 cups, 7 to 9 minutes. Stir in the remaining ½ teaspoon of tarragon. Reduce the heat to medium-low; return the chicken and mushrooms to the Dutch oven and simmer briefly to rewarm, 1 to 2 minutes. Serve.

✳

TRUCS:

USING CANNED REDUCED-SODIUM CHICKEN BROTH IS A MODERN COOK'S ANSWER TO OVER-BUSY SCHEDULES. ALTHOUGH THE BOUILLON DE POULE RECIPE (PAGE 14) WOULD BE THE FIRST CHOICE IN AN IDEAL, SCHEDULE-FREE WORLD, HAVING A CAN OR BOX OF DECENTLY FLAVORED, READY-MADE BROTH ALWAYS IN THE PANTRY IS A STEP TOWARD EASIER COOKING.

WHEN YOU SEE THE WORD *FRICASSEE*, YOU CAN GENERALLY ASSUME THE CHICKEN WILL BE GENTLY SIMMERED WITH A WHITE BROTH AND THEN FINISHED WITH A CREAM-BASED SAUCE. IN THE ORIGINAL VERSIONS, THE MEAT OF A FRICASSEE WAS NEVER BROWNED, BUT IN MORE RECENT RECIPES, THE CHICKEN IS SAUTÉED TO ACHIEVE A GOLDEN COLOR FOR EXTRA FLAVOR.

CHICKEN FRICASSEE
WITH BASIL CREAM

*T*he little corner restaurant 7ème Sud, right off the market street rue Cler, proved to be the inspiration for yet one more recipe for this book.

MAKES 4 SERVINGS

1 tablespoon olive oil

One 3½- to 4-pound chicken, cut into 8 pieces
  (see Note, page 123)

¾ teaspoon salt

⅛ teaspoon freshly ground pepper

¼ cup chopped shallots

1½ teaspoons minced garlic

One 14-ounce can reduced-sodium chicken broth

1 cup raw long-grain rice

½ cup heavy cream

1 tablespoon cornstarch

¼ cup pesto

2 cups lamb's lettuce (mâche) or torn leaf lettuce

½ cup small fresh basil leaves or torn larger leaves

2 medium tomatoes, quartered

Heat the olive oil in a large skillet over medium-high heat. When hot, add the chicken, seasoned with ¼ teaspoon of the salt and the pepper, in batches; sauté until golden brown on both sides, 3 to 5 minutes per side. Remove to a Dutch oven. Add the shallots; sauté until beginning to soften, 2 to 3 minutes. Add the garlic; sauté until fragrant, 30 seconds to 1 minute. Remove to the Dutch oven. Pour off any fat from the skillet. Add the broth; bring to a simmer, scraping up any brown bits from the bottom of the skillet. Pour into the Dutch oven. Bring just to a boil over medium heat; reduce the heat to low. Simmer with the cover just slightly ajar until the chicken is tender and the thighs are no longer pink in the thickest portion when cut with a knife, 50 to 60 minutes. Remove the chicken to a platter; cover with aluminum foil to keep warm.

Meanwhile, cook the rice. Bring 2 cups of water
and the remaining ½ teaspoon of salt to a boil
in a medium saucepan. Add the rice, reduce the
heat to low, and cook, covered, until the rice is
tender and the water is absorbed, 20 to 25
minutes. Turn off the heat and let the rice
stand, covered, until ready to serve.

Increase the heat to high under the Dutch oven;
add the cream and boil until reduced by half,
5 to 8 minutes. Dissolve the cornstarch with
2 tablespoons of water in a small bowl; remove
the cream mixture from the heat and slowly
whisk in the dissolved cornstarch. Return
the cream mixture to the heat and boil until
thickened, 1 to 2 minutes. Remove from the
heat; stir in the pesto.

To serve, mound the rice in the center of a
large, shallow serving bowl; surround with the
chicken. Pour the basil sauce over the chicken.
Arrange the mâche, basil leaves, and tomato
quarters in a ring between the rice and chicken,
overlapping part of the chicken.

TRUC:

PURCHASED PESTO FROM THE REFRIGERATOR
SECTION OF YOUR GROCERY STORE WORKS
VERY WELL IN THIS RECIPE. MAKE SURE TO
BUY A BRAND THAT LISTS BASIL AS THE
FIRST INGREDIENT.

FRICASSÉE DE POULET AU GINGEMBRE MINCEUR
LOW-FAT CHICKEN FRICASSEE WITH GINGER

Although most French recipes follow classic combinations, certain variations crop up from time to time. Using a little fresh ginger is one such departure. This dish includes just the right amount to add a spark of flavor but not enough to drift into the muddled arena of fusion cooking.

MAKES 6 SERVINGS

1 tablespoon canola oil

12 skinless, bone-in chicken thighs

½ teaspoon salt

⅛ teaspoon freshly ground pepper

1½ cups frozen baby onions, thawed

1 cup reduced-sodium chicken broth

½ cup white wine

2 teaspoons minced fresh ginger

¾ cup evaporated skimmed milk

3 tablespoons all-purpose flour

Heat the canola oil in a large skillet over medium-high heat. When hot, add the thighs, seasoned with the salt and pepper, in batches; sauté until golden brown on both sides, 2 to 3 minutes per side. Remove to a Dutch oven. Add the onions; sauté until just beginning to brown, stirring occasionally to turn, 3 to 4 minutes. Add to the Dutch oven along with the broth, the white wine, and 1½ teaspoons of the ginger. Simmer, covered, over low heat until the thighs are fork tender, 50 to 60 minutes. Remove the thighs and onions with a slotted spoon; cover with aluminum foil to keep warm.

Whisk the evaporated skimmed milk into the flour in a small bowl until smooth; whisk into the liquid in the Dutch oven. Increase the heat to medium-high; add the remaining ½ teaspoon of ginger. Bring to a boil; cook until the sauce has thickened slightly, 2 to 3 minutes. Reduce the heat to medium-low; return the thighs to the Dutch oven and simmer briefly to rewarm, 1 to 2 minutes. Serve.

✳

TRUC:

IN A NOD TO *CUISINE MINCEUR*—THE FRENCH VERSION OF LIGHTER COOKING, THIS RECIPE TRIMS ITS FAT CONTENT AND CALORIES BY CALLING FOR EVAPORATED SKIMMED MILK INSTEAD OF HEAVY CREAM AND FOR REMOVING THE CHICKEN SKIN BEFORE COOKING.

MOROCCAN CHICKEN WITH PRESERVED LEMON AND OLIVES

*I*n this stew—really a tagine—cooking stovetop approximates the authentic brazier-based cooking of Morocco, a former French colony, but comes together a bit faster than a traditional version. With its strong lemon-olive flavors, the dish delivers plenty of taste without needing an extended cooking time. Serve this with cooked couscous and a cucumber and tomato salad.

MAKES 6 SERVINGS

2 large garlic cloves, chopped

1 teaspoon ground ginger

¾ teaspoon paprika

¾ teaspoon salt

¼ teaspoon ground cumin

¼ teaspoon freshly ground pepper

1 preserved lemon (see Truc)

3 bone-in, skin-on chicken breasts, cut in half crosswise across the bone

3 bone-in, skin-on chicken thighs

3 bone-in, skin-on chicken drumsticks

2 cups chopped onions

¼ cup chopped fresh cilantro plus ¼ cup whole cilantro leaves

2 tablespoons olive oil

1 cinnamon stick

Pinch saffron, optional

1½ cups pitted kalamata olives

⅓ cup fresh lemon juice

Chop the garlic, ginger, paprika, salt, cumin, and pepper together on a cutting board. Rinse the preserved lemon; cut it in half. Remove the seeds; scoop out the flesh. Reserve the rind. Chop the flesh into the garlic mixture to make a paste.

Arrange the chicken pieces in a single layer in a shallow glass baking dish. Rub the paste into the chicken; refrigerate, covered, to marinate for 3 to 4 hours.

Place the chicken in a Dutch oven with the chicken breast pieces arranged on top of the thighs and drumsticks; top with the onions and chopped cilantro. Add 1½ cups of water, the olive oil, and the cinnamon stick; bring just to a boil over medium heat. Reduce the heat to low; crumble the saffron, if using, into the liquid. Simmer with the cover just slightly ajar until the chicken is tender and the thighs are no longer pink in the thickest portion when cut with a knife, 50 to 60 minutes. Remove the chicken; cover with aluminum foil to keep warm.

Increase the heat to high. Boil the liquid for 10 minutes. Chop the reserved rind from the preserved lemon; add to the liquid along with the olives. Boil for 2 minutes; add the lemon juice. Reduce the heat to medium-low; return the chicken to the Dutch oven and simmer briefly to rewarm, 1 to 2 minutes. Garnish with the cilantro leaves and serve.

TRUC:

ALTHOUGH IT IS POSSIBLE TO BUY PRESERVED LEMONS FROM SPECIALTY SHOPS, I OFTEN MAKE MY OWN. I'VE DEVELOPED THIS METHOD STARTING FROM ONE GIVEN BY PAULA WOLFERT IN HER BOOK *COUSCOUS AND OTHER GOOD FOOD FROM MOROCCO.*

SCORE 6 THIN SLASHES FROM THE TOP TO THE BOTTOM AND PARTIALLY THROUGH THE PEEL OF 2 LEMONS, TRYING NOT TO CUT INTO THE FLESH. PUT ½ CUP OF KOSHER SALT IN A MEDIUM NONREACTIVE SAUCEPAN AND ADD THE LEMONS PLUS ENOUGH WATER TO COVER THEM; BOIL OVER MEDIUM HEAT, TURNING THEM OCCASIONALLY AS THEY BOB TO THE SURFACE, UNTIL THEY ARE VERY SOFT, 15 TO 20 MINUTES.

REMOVE THE LEMONS TO A CLEAN PINT JAR; ADD ENOUGH COOKING LIQUID TO FILL THE JAR. COVER THE JAR WITH A PLASTIC LID (OR PROTECT A METAL LID WITH A DOUBLE LAYER OF PLASTIC WRAP SANDWICHED BETWEEN THE LID AND THE JAR) AND LET THE LEMONS STEEP, REFRIGERATED, FOR AT LEAST 3 DAYS BEFORE USING. THE LEMONS WILL KEEP FOR SEVERAL MONTHS, COVERED WITH BRINE, IN THE REFRIGERATOR.

POTÉE CHAMPENOISE
CHICKEN AND CABBAGE STEW

A potée is an amalgam of soup and stew, offering meat cooked with broth and cabbage, often in a flameproof earthenware container. A potée champenoise is nicknamed the grape-pickers' potée and is distinguished by including celery root and chicken.

MAKES 6 SERVINGS

One 3½- to 4-pound chicken, cut into 8 pieces (see Note, page 123)

5 ounces salt pork strips (lardons), rind removed and cut into 1-inch-long × ¼-inch-thick strips (about ¾ cup)

½ medium cabbage, cored and cut into 1-inch-wide strips

3 carrots, peeled and cut into 2-inch-long pieces

2 medium onions, halved and cut into 1-inch wedges

2 small turnips, peeled and cut into 1-inch wedges

1 small celery root, peeled and cut into 1-inch pieces

1 bouquet garni (2 sprigs parsley, 2 sprigs thyme, and 1 bay leaf, tied together with twine)

Place the chicken in a Dutch oven; sprinkle with the salt pork. Add the cabbage, carrots, onions, turnips, and celery root. Cover with water; add the bouquet garni. Bring just to a boil over medium heat; reduce the heat to low and barely simmer until the chicken and vegetables are meltingly tender, 1½ to 2 hours. Remove the bouquet garni. Place the chicken and vegetables on a serving platter; pour the broth into a soup terrine, if desired. Serve the chicken and vegetables in large shallow bowls, such as soup bowls or pasta dishes, and top with broth.

TRUC:

SALT PORK MAKES A GOOD SUBSTITUTE FOR THE UNSMOKED BACON USED IN FRANCE TO MAKE LARDONS. SO UBIQUITOUS IS THEIR USE THAT LARDONS ARE SOLD, CUT UP, IN SMALL PACKAGES FOR THE COOK'S CONVENIENCE. A BIT FIRMER IN TEXTURE THAN THE FRENCH LARDONS, SALT PORK DOES WELL WHEN SIMMERED.

CHICKEN IN A POT

It was Henry IV, back in the sixteenth century, who first promised his citizens a chicken in every Sunday pot. Long simmered to form a rich broth, this lush poached chicken needs no more than its accompanying vegetables and some crusty, peasant bread to make us understand the significance of Henry's pledge.

MAKES 6 SERVINGS

One 5- to 6-pound chicken

1 pound veal knuckle(s), optional

One-half 12-ounce package breakfast
  sausage links

One 49-ounce can reduced-sodium chicken broth

1 medium onion, halved

4 cloves

1 celery stalk, halved

10 peppercorns

3 sprigs parsley

3 sprigs thyme

1 bay leaf

¾ teaspoon salt

One 1-pound package baby carrots

4 small leeks, white and pale green portions
  only, halved lengthwise, well rinsed, and cut
  into 1½-inch-long pieces

2 medium turnips, peeled and cut into
  1½-inch cubes

Truss the chicken; place in a small, deep stockpot or other flameproof pot large enough to hold all the ingredients but not excessively wide. Add the veal knuckle, if using, and the sausage links. Add the broth and enough cold water to cover, about an additional 6 cups. Bring almost to a boil over medium-high heat (larger bubbles should break the surface around the edges), and reduce the heat to medium-low. Gently simmer for 10 minutes; skim off any surface foam. Add the onion halves stuck with the cloves, the celery, peppercorns, parsley, thyme, bay leaf, and salt. Reduce the heat to low; partially cover and barely simmer for 1 hour (1½ hours if using an older chicken). Remove the chicken, using the trussing strings; let drain over the pot and place on a plate. Strain the broth through several layers of cheesecloth into a large bowl; discard the other poaching meats and vegetables. Return the chicken to the pot; add the carrots, leeks, and turnips. Pour in the strained broth. Heat over medium-high heat until just simmering. Reduce the heat to low and barely simmer with the cover slightly ajar until the vegetables are tender, 30 to 40 minutes. Remove the chicken, slice, and arrange the sliced pieces on a warm platter. Remove the vegetables from the broth with a slotted spoon and surround the chicken with them. Pour the broth into a soup tureen, if desired. Serve the sliced chicken and vegetables in large shallow bowls, such as soup bowls or pasta dishes, and top with broth.

✳

TRUC:

TRADITIONAL POULE AU POT IS OFTEN STUFFED WITH A COMBINATION OF BREAD AND SAUSAGE. BECAUSE THE CHICKEN CAVITY CAN HOLD ONLY A SMALL AMOUNT OF STUFFING, THE REMAINDER NEEDS TO BE WRAPPED IN CABBAGE LEAVES AND POACHED ALONG WITH THE CHICKEN IN THE POT. ALL OF THIS MAKES FOR A FAR MORE COMPLICATED PREPARATION THAN HARRIED COOKS ARE INCLINED TO DO. BY ADDING SOME SAUSAGE LINKS WHILE THE CHICKEN IS SIMMERING, THE BROTH TAKES ON THE SAME WONDERFUL FLAVOR WITHOUT THE FUSS OF MAKING STUFFING. YOU CAN EVEN SAVE THE COOKED SAUSAGES FOR USE ELSEWHERE. CHOP THEM AND ADD THEM TO COUNTRY-STYLE HASH BROWNS OR TO YOUR NEXT SPAGHETTI SAUCE.

CHICKEN MARENGO

*L*egend *attributes this recipe to Napoleon's chef. Following the battle of Marengo, necessity required him to create a meal using local ingredients, including a chicken, a few crayfish or shrimp, and a handful of olives. As with all legends and long-term recipes, this dish has acquired many variations. Sometimes the shrimp are omitted; sometimes the garnish includes deep-fried eggs on butter-sautéed croutons. The eggs are a delightful touch but simply poach them, allowing one per person, for a more modern presentation. Serve them on buttered toast triangles or buttered, toasted French bread circles around the edge of the platter.*

MAKES 6 SERVINGS

2 tablespoons olive oil

3 bone-in, skin-on chicken breasts

3 bone-in, skin-on chicken thighs

3 bone-in, skin-on chicken drumsticks

¾ teaspoon salt

¼ teaspoon freshly ground pepper

¼ cup Cognac

8 ounces white button mushrooms, halved or quartered if large

20 to 24 frozen baby onions, thawed

1 cup white wine

2 cups peeled, chopped fresh tomatoes or one 14.5-ounce can diced tomatoes in juice

1 teaspoon dried thyme

1 teaspoon minced garlic

1 pound raw shelled and deveined large shrimp

¼ teaspoon dried oregano

2 tablespoons all-purpose flour

2 tablespoons salted butter, softened

¾ cup pitted niçoise or kalamata olives

Heat the olive oil in a large skillet over medium-high heat. When hot, add the chicken, seasoned with ¼ teaspoon of the salt and the pepper, in batches; sauté until well browned on both sides, 4 to 5 minutes per side. Pour off any fat from the skillet. Return all the chicken to the skillet; pour the Cognac over the chicken. Immediately light with a match to flame and cook until the flames disappear. Place the mushrooms and onions in the bottom of a Dutch oven; arrange the chicken on top. Add the white wine to the skillet; bring to a simmer, scraping up any brown bits remaining on the bottom of the skillet. Pour into the Dutch oven. Add the chopped tomatoes and ½ teaspoon of the thyme. Bring just to a boil over medium heat; reduce the heat to low. Simmer with the cover just slightly ajar until the chicken is tender and the thighs are no longer pink in the thickest portion when cut with a knife, 45 to 60 minutes.

Mash the garlic with the remaining ½ teaspoon of salt with the tines of a fork on a cutting board to form a paste. Add to the Dutch oven along with the remaining ½ teaspoon of thyme, the shrimp, and the oregano. Simmer until the shrimp are curled, pink, and no longer translucent in the center, 4 to 5 minutes. Remove the chicken and shrimp to a platter; cover with aluminum foil to keep warm.

Blend the flour and butter together with a fork in a small dish to form a paste *(beurre manié)*. Off the heat, whisk the flour mixture into the liquid in bits. Return to high heat; boil until thickened and slightly reduced, 3 to 4 minutes. Pour over the chicken; garnish with the olives.

TRUCS:

USING BEURRE MANIÉ IS A TRADITIONAL FRENCH THICKENING METHOD. BY BLENDING THE FLOUR AND BUTTER TOGETHER AND THEN WHISKING IT IN BY BITS, YOU AVOID FORMING LUMPS.

IF YOU ARE USING CANNED, DICED TOMATOES INSTEAD OF FRESH—A WISE CHOICE DURING THE WINTER MONTHS—USE ABOUT ¼ TEASPOON LESS SALT IN THE TOTAL RECIPE.

CHICKEN WITH PORT

In this old-world classic, chicken starts with a bit of Cognac flamed to seal in flavor, and closes with port and cream for a silky smooth finish.

MAKES 6 SERVINGS

1 tablespoon canola oil

3 bone-in, skin-on chicken breasts, cut in half crosswise across the bone

3 bone-in, skin-on chicken thighs

3 bone-in, skin-on chicken drumsticks

¼ teaspoon salt

⅛ teaspoon freshly ground pepper

½ cup minced shallots

¼ cup Cognac

8 ounces white button mushrooms, quartered

1 cup reduced-sodium chicken broth

½ cup white wine

½ cup port

½ cup heavy cream

1½ tablespoons cornstarch

Heat the canola oil in a large skillet over medium-high heat. When hot, sauté the chicken, seasoned with the salt and pepper, in batches, until well browned on both sides, 4 to 5 minutes per side. Remove. Add the shallots; reduce the heat to medium-low and sauté until just starting to soften, about 2 minutes. Return the chicken to the skillet; pour the Cognac over the chicken. Immediately light with a match to flame and cook until the flames disappear. Place the quartered mushrooms in the bottom of a Dutch oven or large pot; add the chicken, arranging the breast pieces on top of the thighs and drumsticks. Add the broth to the skillet; bring to a simmer over low heat, scraping up any brown bits on the bottom of the skillet. Pour into the Dutch oven along with the white wine. Bring just to a boil over medium heat; reduce the heat to low. Simmer with the cover just slightly ajar until the chicken is tender and the thighs are no longer pink in the thickest portion when cut with a knife, 45 to 60 minutes. Remove the chicken to a platter; cover with aluminum foil to keep warm.

Add all but 2 tablespoons of the port and the cream to the Dutch oven; boil rapidly over high heat to reduce by half, about 10 minutes. Combine the reserved 2 tablespoons of port with the cornstarch in a small dish; slowly whisk into the sauce to thicken. Reduce the heat to medium-low; return the chicken to the Dutch oven and simmer briefly to rewarm, 1 to 2 minutes. Serve.

TRUC:

PORT, LIKE MADEIRA AND SHERRY, IS A FORTIFIED WINE, MEANING THAT EXTRA ALCOHOL IS ADDED TO THE WINE DURING FERMENTATION. THESE WINES ARE USED IN COOKING TO ADD THEIR DISTINCTIVE CHARACTER TO A DISH. AUTHENTIC PORTS, MADE IN PORTUGAL, ARE LABELED "PORTO." ALTHOUGH IT IS NOT NECESSARY TO USE AN EXPENSIVE, AGED VINTAGE PORT, IT IS ALWAYS A GOOD IDEA TO KEEP THE FOLLOWING RULE IN MIND: NEVER COOK WITH A WINE YOU WOULD NOT DRINK.

CHICKEN WITH DRIED PLUMS AND RED WINE

Prunes have a bad rep in the United States—hence their born-again status as dried plums. In France, there is no such image problem. The country knows a good thing when it tastes one, no matter what the name. There's even an area that's famous for its prunes, called Agen. Steeping them in wine and orange zest plumps the prunes wonderfully and they cook to a melting softness as the chicken simmers.

MAKES 4 SERVINGS

16 dried plums (prunes)

2 cups red wine

1 teaspoon grated orange zest

1 tablespoon canola oil

⅓ cup salt pork strips (lardons), about
  ⅜ inch wide

One 3½- to 4-pound cut-up chicken

¼ teaspoon salt

¼ teaspoon freshly ground pepper

1 medium onion, chopped

One 14-ounce can reduced-sodium chicken broth

½ teaspoon dried thyme

Soak the dried plums in a small bowl with 1 cup of the red wine and the orange zest; set aside.

Heat the canola oil in a large skillet over medium heat. When hot, add the lardons and sauté until browned, 4 to 5 minutes. Remove to a Dutch oven. Add the chicken pieces, seasoned with the salt and pepper, in batches; sauté until well browned on both sides, 4 to 5 minutes per side. Remove to the Dutch oven. Add the onion to the skillet; sauté until softened and lightly browned, 4 to 5 minutes. Remove to the Dutch oven. Pour off any fat from the skillet. Add the remaining cup of red wine to the skillet; bring to a simmer, scraping up any brown bits from the pan, 1 to 2 minutes. Pour into the Dutch oven; add the dried plums and the soaking liquid including the orange zest. Pour the broth into the Dutch oven; sprinkle with the thyme. Bring just to a boil over medium heat; reduce the heat to low. Simmer with the cover just slightly ajar until the chicken is tender and the thighs are no longer pink in the thickest portion when cut with a knife, 45 to 60 minutes. Remove the chicken and dried plums; cover with aluminum foil to keep warm.

Increase the heat to high and boil until reduced to 2 cups, about 10 minutes. Reduce the heat to medium-low; return the chicken and dried plums to the Dutch oven and simmer briefly to rewarm, 1 to 2 minutes.

TRUC:

WHEN BUYING DRIED PLUMS, MAKE SURE THEY ARE PLIABLE. ANY DRIED FRUIT OR TOMATO SHOULD BE SUPPLE, NOT RIGID.

POULET AU VINAIGRE

CHICKEN WITH VINEGAR

Although a Lyonnais mainstay, chicken with vinegar is no stranger to menus throughout France. Julia Child supposes, in her book From Julia Child's Kitchen, *that its frequent appearance comes from the increasing use of insipidly flavored chickens. I think the recipe's popularity comes from the fact that it simply tastes so good. Although the earthy vinegar flavor may indeed help a lackluster bird along, it also makes a good one even better.*

MAKES 4 SERVINGS

1 tablespoon canola oil

1 tablespoon salted butter

One 3½- to 4-pound cut-up chicken

¼ teaspoon salt

⅛ teaspoon freshly ground pepper

½ cup chopped shallots

1 tablespoon tomato paste

1 large garlic clove, minced

½ cup aged or best-quality red wine vinegar

3 sprigs thyme

2 sprigs tarragon

1 cup white wine

1 cup reduced-sodium chicken broth

¼ cup heavy cream

2 tablespoons chopped fresh parsley for garnish

Heat the canola oil and butter in a large skillet over medium-high heat. When sizzling, add the chicken, seasoned with the salt and pepper, in batches; sauté until well browned on both sides, 3 to 4 minutes per side. Remove to a Dutch oven. Reduce the heat to medium and add the shallots and tomato paste. Cook, stirring often, to soften slightly, 1 to 2 minutes; add the garlic and cook until fragrant, 30 seconds to 1 minute. Add about half the red wine vinegar; cook for 1 minute. Add the remainder; cook for an additional minute. Pour into the Dutch oven; add the thyme and tarragon. Bring to a simmer over medium heat; cook for about 3 minutes. Turn the chicken and cook for an additional 3 minutes to allow the vinegar to permeate the other side. Add the white wine and broth; bring just to a boil. Reduce the heat to low. Simmer with the cover slightly ajar until the chicken is tender and the thighs are no longer pink in the thickest portion when cut with a knife, 45 to 60 minutes. Remove the chicken to a platter; cover with aluminum foil to keep warm. Discard the thyme and tarragon sprigs.

Increase the heat to high; reduce the liquid by half to thicken slightly and concentrate the flavors, 5 to 8 minutes. Whisk in the cream; boil to reduce slightly, 2 to 3 minutes. Reduce the heat to medium-low; return the chicken to the Dutch oven and simmer briefly to rewarm, 1 to 2 minutes. Return the chicken to the platter; pour the sauce over all. Garnish with the parsley and serve.

TRUC:

AGED RED WINE VINEGAR IS KEPT IN OAK JUST LIKE WINE TO MELLOW AND ENHANCE ITS ZESTY TANG. IF DIFFICULT TO FIND, USE THE BEST-QUALITY RED WINE VINEGAR AVAILABLE.

CHICKEN WATERZOOI

*B*elgium shares a northern border with France and shares recipes as well. My Belgian cousin Joseph introduced me to this dish in Brussels, but it is served in northern France as well. Laced with cream and enriched with an egg yolk, it's just the thing to raise the spirits on a drizzly, gray-skied day, so common in the region.

MAKES 6 SERVINGS

Two 14-ounce cans reduced-sodium chicken broth

2 pounds boneless, skinless chicken thighs,
   cut in half

1 medium onion

2 cloves

1 celery stalk, coarsely chopped

1 large carrot, coarsely chopped

5 sprigs parsley

1 bay leaf

½ teaspoon dried thyme

4 tablespoons (½ stick) salted butter

2 medium leeks, white and pale green portions
   only, halved lengthwise, well rinsed, and cut
   into 2-inch-long matchsticks (julienne)

1 large carrot, cut into 2-inch-long
   matchsticks (julienne)

1 large celery stalk, cut into 2-inch-long
   matchsticks (julienne)

⅓ cup all-purpose flour

½ cup heavy cream

1 egg yolk

Put the broth, chicken, onion stuck with the cloves, chopped celery, chopped carrot, parsley sprigs, bay leaf, and thyme in a large saucepan. Bring just to a boil over medium heat; reduce the heat to low. Simmer until the chicken is tender, about 45 minutes.

During the last 20 minutes of cooking, melt the butter over low heat in a Dutch oven. Add the julienned vegetables and cover. Continue to cook until the vegetables are soft and tender, stirring occasionally, about 20 minutes. Remove the cover and stir in the flour. Strain the chicken cooking liquid into the Dutch oven and whisk to combine. Increase the heat to medium and bring to a boil. Boil until thickened, 2 to 3 minutes. Add the chicken, discarding the remaining poaching vegetables. Whisk together the cream and egg yolk. Remove the Dutch oven from the heat and whisk in the cream mixture. Return to low heat briefly to thicken slightly but do not boil, 1 to 2 minutes. Serve.

✳

TRUC:

ADDING AN EGG YOLK TO A SAUCE AT THE END OF THE COOKING PROCESS IS A CLASSIC TECHNIQUE. IT ADDS A VELVETY BODY TO THE POACHING LIQUID ALREADY THICKENED WITH FLOUR. IT IS CRITICAL NOT TO BOIL THE SAUCE ONCE THE YOLK IS ADDED OR IT WILL CURDLE.

Un Oeuf Is Enough

Egg Dishes

BISTRO SALAD

This wonderful salad, originally from Lyon, plays with flavors in the most satisfying way. Combining the slight bitterness of frisée lettuce with the saltiness of bacon and the tartness of vinegar and mustard, the salad is anointed with the delicate richness of a perfectly poached egg. As the yolk breaks and mingles with the other ingredients, everything pulls together into one delightful whole.

MAKES 4 SERVINGS

¼ cup best-quality red wine vinegar

1½ teaspoons Dijon mustard

⅛ teaspoon salt

⅛ teaspoon freshly ground pepper

¼ pound thick-cut bacon, cut into ¼-inch-wide strips (lardons; 3 to 4 slices)

Canola oil

2 teaspoons minced garlic

12 cups torn frisée lettuce, if available, or torn curly endive or escarole leaves

4 large eggs

Whisk 3 tablespoons of the red wine vinegar with the mustard, salt, and pepper together in a small bowl; set aside.

Fill a large skillet (to be used for poaching the eggs) about three-fourths full of water; add the remaining 1 tablespoon of vinegar. Bring to a simmer over medium-low heat and keep at a simmer.

Meanwhile, cook the bacon in a medium skillet over medium heat until browned and crispy, 6 to 8 minutes. Remove; drain on paper towels. Pour the bacon fat into a measuring cup; add enough canola oil to measure 6 tablespoons. Return the bacon fat and oil to the skillet. Heat over low heat; add the garlic. Cook the garlic until fragrant, 30 seconds to 1 minute. Add the vinegar-mustard mixture; continue cooking, whisking to blend, to mellow the vinegar, about 1 minute. Immediately pour the dressing over the frisée in a large bowl; toss to coat. Divide the frisée among four salad plates; sprinkle with the bacon.

Crack the eggs, one at a time, into a custard cup and then slide each egg into the simmering water. Poach until the whites are set but the yolks are still soft, 4 to 5 minutes. Remove with a slotted spoon and place one poached egg on top of each salad.

TRUC:

ADDING A BIT OF VINEGAR TO THE POACHING LIQUID HELPS HOLD THE EGGS TOGETHER. THE YOLKS ARE LESS LIKELY TO BREAK AND THE WHITE IS LESS LIKELY TO SPREAD IN TENDRILS WHEN COOKED. THE ACIDIC, VINEGAR-LACED WATER HELPS THE EGGS COOK FASTER AND THEREFORE KEEP FROM SPREADING TOO MUCH. THIS KEEPS THEM PLUMPER AND CONTAINS THE WHITES AS THEY POACH. SO DOES PLACING THEM IN A SMALL DISH AND SLIDING THEM INTO THE SIMMERING WATER JUST ABOVE THE SURFACE. USE THE FRESHEST OF EGGS FOR THE NICEST SHAPE.

CURRIED CHICKEN CLAFOUTI

Clafoutis *are normally homey, egg-based batter desserts, often baked with cherries or other fruits. This fanciful adaptation uses the batter in a savory application and puts leftover chicken to excellent use.*

MAKES 4 MAIN COURSE SERVINGS OR 6 LUNCHEON SERVINGS

1½ cups diced cooked chicken

¼ cup chopped green onion

2 tablespoons raisins

½ cup all-purpose flour

1½ teaspoons mild curry powder

½ teaspoon salt

⅛ teaspoon freshly ground pepper

1½ cups half-and-half

4 large eggs, lightly beaten

Preheat the oven to 400°F. Butter a deep-dish glass or ceramic pie pan or a 1½-quart baking dish. Sprinkle the chicken, green onion, and raisins in the bottom of the pan.

Mix the flour, curry powder, salt, and pepper together in a medium bowl. Slowly whisk in the half-and-half until blended; whisk in the eggs until blended. Pour over the chicken mixture in the pan.

Bake for 40 to 45 minutes or until puffed, browned, and set. Cut in wedges and serve.

TRUC:

TRY CREATING YOUR OWN CLAFOUTI BY
CHANGING THE INGREDIENTS IN THIS DISH.
FOR EXAMPLE, USE DICED, OVEN-DRIED
TOMATOES INSTEAD OF RAISINS AND SPRINKLE
THE CHICKEN WITH A HANDFUL OF CHOPPED
FRESH BASIL FOR SEASONING INSTEAD OF
USING CURRY POWDER.

LAYERED PROVENÇAL OMELET

The day after buying our new home in France, we headed to nearby Buis les Baronnies to establish our house insurance through the local bank. After struggling for an hour with unfamiliar French vocabulary, we decided lunch was next on the priority list. Eggs seemed just the soothing thing we needed after the rigors of dealing with all that paperwork. That's how I discovered crespéou, *a delightful layered omelet concoction, typical of Provence.*

MAKES 4 SERVINGS

¼ cup extra virgin olive oil

9 large eggs

3 tablespoons milk

Freshly ground pepper

½ cup diced roasted red bell pepper (from a jar)

2 tablespoons chopped green onion

⅛ teaspoon salt

½ teaspoon herbes de Provence

2 tablespoons pitted, chopped Nyons or
  kalamata olives, patted dry

¼ cup chopped marinated artichokes (from a jar),
  patted dry

Preheat the oven to 350°F. Grease the bottom and the sides of a 9- to 10-inch pie pan with 1 tablespoon of the olive oil.

Break 3 eggs in each of 3 bowls. Add 1 tablespoon of milk and several grinds of pepper to each bowl (about ⅛ teaspoon of pepper per bowl); whisk each until combined. Stir the bell pepper, green onion, and salt into the first bowl. Stir the herbes de Provence into the second bowl.

Heat 1 tablespoon of the olive oil in a medium-sized, nonstick skillet over medium heat. When hot, add the bell pepper–egg mixture. Cook, pushing the eggs with a spatula or fork toward the center as they set and tilting the pan so the uncooked eggs flow to the sides. While the top of the omelet is still slightly undercooked, slide the omelet into the prepared pie pan. Add 1 tablespoon of olive oil to the same skillet. When hot, stir the olives into the eggs mixed with the herbes de Provence. Repeat the omelet-making procedure and slide the omelet on top of the bell pepper omelet. Add the last tablespoon of olive oil to the skillet. When hot, add the third bowl of eggs to the skillet; repeat the omelet-making procedure. Scatter the chopped artichokes over the omelet and slide on top of the olive omelet. Place the pie pan in the oven and bake for 4 to 6 minutes or until the eggs are set. Remove from the oven. Place a serving plate over the pie pan and invert the layered omelets onto the plate, with the red bell pepper omelet on top. Cut into 4 wedges and serve.

TRUC:

ONCE THE JARS ARE OPENED, STORE THEIR REMAINING CONTENTS (ROASTED PEPPERS, PITTED KALAMATA OLIVES, AND MARINATED ARTICHOKES) IN THE REFRIGERATOR AND USE TO ADD FLAVOR TO PIZZAS, SALADS, AND PASTA DISHES.

LAIT DE POULE

EGGNOG

Lait de poule *literally translates as "milk of the hen," an amusing name for a warming drink I enjoyed during my student days at the Sorbonne. On damply cold winter evenings so frequent in Paris, my friends and I would sometimes visit a small café/bar on the boulevard St. Germain that specialized in rum drinks. Since the Caribbean islands of Martinique and Guadeloupe are departments of France and manufacturers of quality rum, a café like this was a logical place to celebrate a fine French product. There, we would order hot milk punches laced with lemon as well as spirits, letting their gentle heat chase away the chill while we discussed class assignments or weekend plans.*

MAKES 1 SERVING

1 large egg yolk

1 tablespoon light brown sugar

1 cup milk

1 strip lemon peel

1 cinnamon stick, optional

2 tablespoons dark rum

Whisk the egg yolk and brown sugar together in a small bowl until well blended. Heat the milk, lemon peel, and cinnamon stick, if using, in a small saucepan over medium-low heat until just boiling. Remove the lemon peel and cinnamon stick. Whisk about one-fourth of the milk into the egg yolk mixture until combined; whisk the yolk mixture into the remaining milk in the pan. Return to the heat, stirring gently with a spoon, until the foam begins to subside and the mixture thickens slightly, 1 to 2 minutes. Do not boil or the mixture will curdle. Immediately pour into a mug; add the rum and stir.

TRUCS:

Traditionally this recipe is finished when the hot milk and egg mixture are whisked together. In these days of salmonella contamination, returning the milk and egg mixture to the heat ensures that the beverage will reach the safe temperature of 160°F. Make sure to stir the *lait de poule* with a spoon, not a whisk, during the final heating. The disappearing bubbles are a sign the mixture is hot enough; if you continue using a whisk, you generate more bubbles, missing this helpful signal and running the risk of accidentally overheating the mixture.

This comforting beverage can also be served to children, sans rum. For a kid-pleasing variation, try it using chocolate milk and omit the brown sugar.

OEUFS EN COCOTTE

SHIRRED EGGS

S mall Parisian restaurants have discovered the American concept of Sunday brunch. Latching on to the idea of serving eggs to hungry diners, they have a wealth of traditional recipes. These little dishes, quickly prepared and quickly baked, are soothingly rich and satisfying as a midmorning offering to appease late-rising appetites.

MAKES 4 SERVINGS

¼ cup chopped chives
¼ teaspoon salt
Pinch cayenne
4 large eggs
¼ cup heavy cream

Preheat the oven to 350°F. Line the bottom of a 13 × 9-inch baking pan with a dishcloth or towel.

Place 1 tablespoon of chives in the bottom of each of four 6-ounce ramekins or custard cups. Blend the salt and cayenne together; sprinkle equally over the chives in the ramekins. Add an egg to each ramekin; pour 1 tablespoon of cream over each egg. Place the ramekins in the prepared pan on top of the dishcloth; pour boiling water to the depth of ½ inch into the pan. Bake for 12 to 14 minutes, until the whites are just set and the yolks are filmed but still runny. Serve immediately.

TRUC:

NORMALLY, FOODS COOK IN THE OVEN FROM
THE OUTSIDE INWARD. WITH DELICATE
INGREDIENTS SUCH AS EGGS, THIS CAN BE A
PROBLEM. ADDING WATER TO THE BAKING PAN
NEUTRALIZES SOME OF THE OVEN'S HEAT ON
THE OUTSIDE SURFACE AND HELPS KEEP THE
EDGES OF THE EGG FROM OVERCOOKING
BEFORE THE CENTER IS SET. LINING THE
BOTTOM OF THE PAN WITH A DISHCLOTH OR
TOWEL DRAWS THE PROTECTIVE WATER UNDER
THE RAMEKINS AND INSULATES THEM FROM
DIRECT CONTACT WITH THE BAKING PAN.

BURGUNDY EGGS IN A
RED WINE SAUCE

---

*T*his recipe is yet another demonstration of what bistro cooking is all about—taking humble ingredients and combining them for optimum flavor until the sum is far greater than its parts. Here the French gild the simple poached egg in much the same way as we do with our eggs Benedict, using a rich, wine-based sauce instead of a butter-based hollandaise.

MAKES 4 SERVINGS

3 tablespoons salted butter, softened

2 tablespoons all-purpose flour

¼ cup thick-cut bacon cut into ¼-inch
   strips (lardons)

2 tablespoons minced shallots

1 cup reduced-sodium beef broth

1 cup red wine

⅛ teaspoon freshly ground pepper

1 tablespoon white wine vinegar

½ teaspoon Kitchen Bouquet

4 large eggs

4 buttered, toasted triangles of white toasting
   bread or 4 slices French bread

Blend 2 tablespoons of the butter and the flour together with a fork to form a paste (beurre manié); set aside.

Heat a medium saucepan over medium heat; add the remaining tablespoon of butter. When sizzling, add the bacon strips; sauté until the bacon begins to color, 2 to 3 minutes. Add the shallots; sauté until softened and browned, stirring often, 3 to 4 minutes. Add the beef broth, red wine, and pepper; simmer for 15 minutes to blend flavors and reduce.

While simmering the wine mixture, fill a large skillet (for poaching the eggs) about three-fourths full of water; add the white wine vinegar. Bring to a simmer over medium-low heat and keep at a simmer.

When the wine mixture has finished simmering,
stir in the Kitchen Bouquet and remove from
the heat. Whisk in the beurre manié in bits.
Return to high heat and boil for 5 minutes to
thicken and reduce.

Crack the eggs, one at a time, into a custard
cup and slide into the simmering vinegar water.
Poach until the whites are set and the yolks are
still soft, 4 to 5 minutes. Remove with a slotted
spoon. Place each on top of a buttered toast
triangle in a ramekin or on a plate. Strain the
sauce and pour over the eggs.

TRUC:

USING A TINY AMOUNT OF KITCHEN BOUQUET
REMOVES THE PURPLE HUE FROM THIS RED
WINE-BASED SAUCE AND GIVES IT A RICH
BROWN CAST WITHOUT AFFECTING FLAVOR.

FRENCH DEVILED EGGS

*M*imosas are delicate yellow flowers that lend their name to dishes using sieved or mashed hard-cooked egg yolk. Most commonly, the term describes egg yolks sprinkled over a salad or mashed and stuffed into hard-cooked egg whites. While we think of deviled eggs as an appetizer, the French also enjoy them as a first course or starter. Try this zesty version either way.

MAKES 6 SERVINGS

6 large eggs

¼ cup mayonnaise

2 teaspoons Dijon mustard

½ teaspoon dry mustard

2 tablespoons minced chives

1 teaspoon finely chopped fresh tarragon

⅛ teaspoon salt

Pinch white pepper

6 lettuce leaves

Place the eggs, in their shells, in a saucepan; cover with water. Heat over medium heat until the water just comes to a boil. Reduce the heat to medium-low, or until just barely boiling, and cook for 12 minutes. Remove from the heat and drain. Immediately cover with cold water. Let cool, changing the water as necessary to keep cold. Tap the shells all over to finely crack; remove the shells. Slice in half lengthwise; remove the yolks.

Mash the yolks with the mayonnaise and mustards to form a smooth, creamy paste. Stir in 1 tablespoon of the chives, the tarragon, salt, and white pepper. Mound into the whites, filling the cavities. Sprinkle with the remaining chives. Place a lettuce leaf on each of six salad plates; top with two filled halves.

TRUC:

UNLIKELY AS IT SEEMS, IN THIS RECIPE, LESS FRESH IS BETTER. TRY TO HARD-COOK EGGS THAT ARE CLOSE TO THE EXPIRATION DATE ON THEIR CARTON; THE SHELLS ARE MUCH EASIER TO REMOVE ON OLDER EGGS. MAKE SURE TO IMMEDIATELY COVER THE COOKED EGGS WITH COLD WATER AND KEEP THE WATER COOL. THIS STOPS THE YOLKS FROM OVERCOOKING AND KEEPS THEM FROM TURNING GREEN.

COUNTRY-STYLE OMELET

Brayaude *is one of those French cooking terms that is code for the regional source of a dish. In this case the area is the Auvergne, known for its ham. Other areas of France prepare very similar ingredients and serve them under the name of* omelette fermière, *indicating the rustic, hearty character of the dish.*

MAKES 4 SERVINGS

8 large eggs
2 tablespoons heavy cream
¼ teaspoon salt
⅛ teaspoon freshly ground pepper
4 tablespoons (½ stick) salted butter
¾ cup diced cooked new potatoes or
 fingerling potatoes

½ cup minced shallots
½ cup smoked chicken, diced ham, turkey,
 Canadian bacon, or pancetta
2 ounces diced Emmentaler or Gruyère cheese
 (about ½ cup)
1 tablespoon chopped fresh chives
1 tablespoon chopped fresh parsley

Whisk the eggs, cream, salt, and pepper together in a medium bowl until just frothy; set aside.

Heat the butter in a large, nonstick skillet over medium heat. When sizzling, add the potatoes, shallots, and chicken; sauté until the potatoes are golden brown, 5 to 8 minutes. Add the egg mixture; cook, pushing the eggs with a spatula or fork toward the center as they set and tilting the pan so the uncooked eggs flow to the sides. When almost set, sprinkle with the cheese. Reduce the heat to medium-low; cover and cook until the eggs are set and the cheese is beginning to melt, 2 to 4 minutes. Sprinkle with the chives and parsley. Slide onto a serving platter or serve from the skillet, cut into wedges.

TRUC:

SOMETIMES USING SMOKED CHICKEN OR TURKEY CAN GIVE A BETTER TEXTURE THAN OVERLY PROCESSED HAM. BUY WHATEVER MOST CLOSELY RESEMBLES A REAL MEAT PRODUCT AND NOT A SLICK, RUBBERY, MOISTURE-INJECTED IMPOSTER.

Jam Omelet

This small brunch or dessert omelet combines the savory taste of eggs and the sweet, fruity taste of preserves in one simple treatment. The recipe can easily be multiplied by the number of people you want to feed because it comes together so quickly. Make the omelets to order, letting your delighted guests choose from a variety of preserves and jams.

MAKES 1 SERVING

2 large eggs

1 tablespoon cream

1 tablespoon salted butter

2 tablespoons preserves or jam

1 tablespoon liqueur, optional

Whisk the eggs and cream together in a small bowl. Heat the butter in a small omelet pan over medium heat. When sizzling, add the eggs. Reduce the heat to medium-low; cook, pushing the eggs with a spatula or fork toward the center as they set and tilting the pan so the uncooked eggs flow to the sides, until almost set, 2 to 3 minutes. Spoon the preserves down the center of the omelet. Flip one side over the other; remove from the heat. If desired, pour the liqueur over the omelet and immediately flame with a match. When the flame extinguishes, cover and let rest for 1 minute or until the eggs are just set. Serve immediately.

TRUC:

I HAVE A SMALL WELL-SEASONED SKILLET
WITH ROUNDED, SLOPING SIDES THAT I LIKE
TO USE FOR OMELETS. I TRY TO KEEP IT JUST
FOR THIS USE AND QUICKLY AND GENTLY
WASH IT AFTERWARD TO MAINTAIN THE
SEASONING. ANOTHER OPTION IS TO USE A
SMALL, NONSTICK SKILLET WITH SOME
WEIGHT TO IT TO MAINTAIN EVEN COOKING.

OMELETTE DE LA MÈRE POULARD

OVEN-BAKED OMELET

The name of this recipe literally translates as "Mother Hen's Omelet." Its namesake, Mère Poulard, ran an inn with her husband at Mont Saint-Michel in Normandy. Although Mère Poulard died long ago, her omelet is still served (for a small fortune) in the inn's restaurant. The secret to her ethereal souffléed eggs involves beating them madly with whisks in copper bowls, making for a rhythmic racket in this touristy spot. My version involves separating some of the eggs and whisking the whites to achieve the extra volume of the original. Without access to the open hearth of the Hôtel Poulard, where the omelets are cooked in long-handled pans by women in regional costumes, I've started this omelet on the stove and finished it in the oven.

MAKES 4 SERVINGS

8 large eggs
2 tablespoons heavy cream
¼ teaspoon salt
⅛ teaspoon freshly ground pepper
½ teaspoon cream of tartar
2 tablespoons salted butter
1 tablespoon chopped fresh parsley

Preheat the oven to 375°F.

Combine 4 whole eggs and 4 yolks in a medium bowl. Beat, using a hand mixer on medium speed, until almost tripled in volume and frothy, 3 to 4 minutes. Stir in the cream, salt, and pepper.

Beat the 4 remaining egg whites in a medium bowl, using a hand mixer with clean beaters, on medium speed until frothy; beat in the cream of tartar. Increase the speed to high; beat until the peaks are almost stiff. (The tips will still dip slightly when the beater is raised.) Stir one-fourth of the whites into the egg mixture to lighten; fold in the remainder.

Immediately heat the butter in a large, oven-proof skillet over medium-high heat and swirl to coat the entire pan. When sizzling, pour in the egg mixture. Bake for 7 to 9 minutes, until the eggs are puffed and just set. Fold in half; slide onto a serving platter. Sprinkle with the parsley and serve immediately.

TRUC:

MAKE SURE WHEN BEATING THE EGG WHITES THAT THERE IS NO GREASE PRESENT ON THE BOWL OR BEATERS TO PREVENT THE WHITES FROM FORMING PEAKS. SINCE SPECKS OF EGG YOLK WILL CAUSE THE SAME PROBLEM, SEPARATE THE EGGS INDIVIDUALLY OVER A SMALL DISH AND THEN ADD THE WHITES, ONE AT A TIME, TO THE MIXING BOWL. THAT WAY, IF A YOLK BREAKS, YOU'VE SPOILED ONLY ONE WHITE INSTEAD OF ALL OF THEM.

OMELETTE À LA SANCERRE

WILD MUSHROOM OMELET

If I come in on the early flight to Paris, I head for a soothing omelet at Sancerre, a charming wine bar in the seventh arrondissement. Depending on the season, they offer luscious, buttery omelets filled with whatever mushrooms are available in the local markets. In early September, when I am often there, the girolles are plentiful. Later in the month, the cèpes (what the Italians call porcini) begin to appear.

MAKES 2 SERVINGS

2 tablespoons salted butter

2 tablespoons chopped shallots

4 ounces wild mushrooms, coarsely chopped,
  such as chanterelles (girolles), porcini (cèpes), or
  oyster mushrooms

¼ teaspoon plus ⅛ teaspoon salt

¼ cup white or red Sancerre wine, or other white
  or red wine, or water

6 large eggs

⅛ teaspoon freshly ground pepper

Heat 1 tablespoon of the butter in a medium skillet over medium heat. When sizzling, add the shallots; sauté for 1 minute. Add the mushrooms; sauté for 2 minutes. Reduce the heat to medium-low; sprinkle with the ¼ teaspoon of salt and sauté until the shallots begin to soften, 2 to 3 minutes. Add the wine and simmer until all the liquid is evaporated and the mushrooms are tender, 4 to 6 minutes. Set aside.

Whisk the eggs, the ⅛ teaspoon of salt, and the pepper in a medium bowl until frothy. Heat the remaining 1 tablespoon of butter in a medium nonstick skillet over medium heat. When sizzling, add the eggs. Reduce the heat to medium-low; cook, pushing the eggs with a spatula or fork toward the center as they set and tilting the pan so the uncooked eggs flow to the sides, until almost set, 3 to 4 minutes. Spoon the cooked mushrooms down the center of the omelet. Flip one side over the other; remove from the heat. Cover and let rest until the eggs are set, 2 to 4 minutes. Divide in two; serve immediately.

✳

TRUC:

COVERING THE OMELET ONCE IT'S OFF THE HEAT AND LETTING IT REST ENSURES THE EGGS ARE COOKED THROUGH WITHOUT ENDING UP OVERLY DRY. THE CONSISTENCY IS A BIT FIRMER THAN THE SLIGHTLY RUNNY, OR *BAVEUSE*, FINISHED OMELET ONE FINDS IN FRANCE, BUT OUR EGGS FACE A POTENTIAL FOR SALMONELLA CONTAMINATION THAT IS NOT COMMON IN FRENCH EGGS. FROM A FOOD SAFETY PERSPECTIVE, COOKING OMELETS A BIT MORE IN THE STATES IS A GOOD IDEA. IF PASTEURIZED EGGS ARE AVAILABLE IN YOUR PART OF THE COUNTRY, USE THEM INSTEAD. THEY WON'T NEED TO BE COVERED AT THE END, AS THE PASTEURIZATION ELIMINATES ANY CONTAMINATION.

BASQUE OPEN-FACED OMELET

This is perhaps the definitive egg dish of the Basque region separating France and Spain. I've been teaching my students this recipe since I began giving cooking lessons more than twenty-five years ago, and everyone loves the combination of salty ham, sautéed vegetables, and the slightest hint of spicy heat from the piment d'Espelette or cayenne.

MAKES 4 SERVINGS

8 large eggs

¼ teaspoon salt

¼ teaspoon piment d'Espelette or pinch cayenne

3 tablespoons olive oil

1 medium onion, chopped (about ¾ cup)

1 green bell pepper, cored and chopped
   (about ¾ cup)

1 large garlic clove, minced (about 1½ teaspoons)

2 medium tomatoes, chopped (about 1 cup)

½ cup diced ham

Beat the eggs, salt, and piment d'Espelette until frothy; set aside.

Heat 2 tablespoons of the olive oil in a large nonstick skillet over medium-high heat. When hot, add the onion and bell pepper; sauté until starting to soften, 2 to 3 minutes. Add the garlic; cook until fragrant, 30 seconds to 1 minute. Add the tomatoes and ham; cook until all the liquid has evaporated, 4 to 5 minutes. Remove to a bowl; wipe the skillet clean. Heat the remaining 1 tablespoon of olive oil. When hot, add the eggs; cook, pushing the eggs with a spatula or fork toward the center as they set and tilting the pan so the uncooked eggs flow to the sides, until almost set, 4 to 5 minutes. When almost set, top with the warm tomato-ham mixture. Reduce the heat to medium-low; cover and cook until the eggs are set, 1 to 3 minutes.

Slide onto a serving platter. Cut into wedges to serve.

TRUC:

MAKE SURE TO CHOOSE THE REDDEST, RIPEST TOMATOES POSSIBLE WHEN PREPARING THIS RECIPE. DON'T FORGET TO CHECK OUT THE ROMA TOMATOES IF THE REGULAR VARIETY IS A SICKLY AND NOT A VIBRANT SHADE. ROMAS ARE OFTEN A BETTER CHOICE IN THE PRODUCE DEPARTMENT, PARTICULARLY DURING THE WINTER MONTHS.

QUICHE AUX ÉPINARDS ET AUX CHAMPIGNONS
SPINACH AND MUSHROOM QUICHE

The name quiche, *derived from the German word* Kuchen, *or cake, has come to mean an egg-based tart throughout France. While the traditional quiche from Lorraine consists simply of eggs, cream, and bacon in a pastry crust, variations like this one are almost as classic. I've added more filling than is typical in this hearty version, making it a good brunch choice or a wonderful appetizer when cut into small squares.*

MAKES 16 APPETIZER SERVINGS, OR 6 FIRST COURSE OR BRUNCH SERVINGS, OR 4 MAIN COURSE SERVINGS

CRUST

1¼ cups all-purpose flour

¼ teaspoon salt

8 tablespoons (1 stick) cold unsalted butter, cut into bits

FILLING

2 tablespoons salted butter

¼ cup minced shallots

8 ounces white button mushrooms, sliced

¼ cup Madeira

One 9-ounce package frozen chopped spinach, thawed

3 large eggs

⅓ cup heavy cream

⅓ cup milk

½ teaspoon salt

⅛ teaspoon freshly ground pepper

4 ounces shredded Gruyère cheese (about 1 cup)

For the crust, combine the flour and salt in a bowl. Cut in the butter with your fingertips or a pastry cutter until the mixture resembles a combination of coarse sand and small pebbles. Toss with 3 to 4 tablespoons of ice water, using just enough water to bring the mixture together in a ball. Wrap in plastic wrap, flatten into a disk, and refrigerate for 1 hour.

Preheat the oven to 425°F. Roll out the dough on a lightly floured surface to a scant ¼-inch thickness. Place the dough in a 9-inch tart pan with a removable bottom. Press the dough downward around the edges to firm the sides. Trim the excess dough and reserve the scraps. Line the dough with aluminum foil; weight the bottom with dried beans, rice, or pie weights. Bake for 12 to 14 minutes, until the dough is set. Remove the foil and weights; bake for an additional 4 to 6 minutes, until just barely colored. If the dough has cracked during baking, let the crust cool slightly, then patch it using some of the reserved scraps of dough, pressing small pieces of the scraps gently into the cracks.

For the filling, while the crust is baking, heat the butter in a large skillet over medium heat. When sizzling, add the shallots. Sauté until softened, 3 to 4 minutes. Add the mushrooms; sauté until tender, 5 to 8 minutes. Add the Madeira; continue to cook until all the liquid has evaporated. Remove from the heat. Squeeze all the moisture from the thawed spinach; stir into the mushrooms to form a rough mixture.

Reduce the oven temperature to 375°F. Place the tart pan in a foil-lined, shallow baking pan. Spoon the spinach-mushroom mixture into the crust. Whisk the eggs together until foamy; whisk in the cream, milk, salt, and pepper. Pour the egg mixture slowly into the quiche pan to fill it completely. Some of the spinach mixture may protrude above the liquid. Sprinkle the cheese over all. Bake for 25 to 30 minutes or until a knife inserted in the center comes out clean.

✳

TRUC:

ADDING A SMALL QUANTITY OF MADEIRA DEEPENS AND ROUNDS THE FLAVORS IN MANY RECIPES. USE A SPLASH IN SAUCES OR GRAVIES WHEN THEY NEED A LITTLE SOMETHING EXTRA. BECAUSE MADEIRA IS A FORTIFIED WINE, IT HAS A LONG SHELF LIFE AND MAKES A HANDY PANTRY ADDITION.

QUICHE AU POULET ET AUX ASPERGES
CHICKEN AND ASPARAGUS QUICHE

When I do food tours in Paris, we begin our days on rue Cler, a charming market street not far from the Eiffel Tower. Small shops line the street, including Tarte Julie, which specializes in quiches. Offering both savory and sweet fillings, they remind me just how good a slice of quiche can be for lunch or a simple supper. This recipe is a great way to use up leftover chicken and turn it into a completely new creation.

MAKES 6 FIRST COURSE OR LUNCHEON SERVINGS OR 4 MAIN COURSE SERVINGS

CRUST

1¼ cups all-purpose flour

¼ teaspoon salt

8 tablespoons (1 stick) cold unsalted butter,
   cut into bits

FILLING

16 thin asparagus spears

1 cup diced cooked chicken

3 ounces Gruyère cheese, shredded (about ¾ cup)

1 ounce Parmigiano-Reggiano cheese, grated
   (about ¼ cup)

¼ cup chopped chives

3 large eggs

½ cup heavy cream

½ cup milk

½ teaspoon salt

¼ teaspoon freshly ground pepper

⅛ teaspoon nutmeg

For the crust, combine the flour and salt in a bowl. Cut in the butter with your fingertips or a pastry cutter until the mixture resembles a combination of coarse sand and small pebbles. Toss with 3 to 4 tablespoons of ice water, using just enough water to bring the mixture together in a ball. Wrap in plastic wrap, flatten into a disk, and refrigerate for 1 hour.

Preheat the oven to 425°F. Roll out the dough on a lightly floured surface to a scant ¼-inch thickness. Place the dough in a 9-inch tart pan with a removable bottom. Press the dough downward around the edges to firm the sides. Trim the excess dough and reserve the scraps. Line the dough with aluminum foil; weight the bottom with dried beans, rice, or pie weights. Bake for 12 to 14 minutes, until the dough is set. Remove the foil and weights; bake for an additional 4 to 6 minutes, until just barely colored. If the dough has cracked during baking, let the crust cool slightly, then patch it using some of the reserved scraps of dough, pressing small pieces of the scraps gently into the cracks.

For the filling, while the crust is baking, trim the asparagus. Trim the tips of 8 spears into 4-inch lengths; cut the remaining portion of those spears and all the remaining spears into 1-inch pieces. Blanch in boiling water for 2 minutes; drain. Run under cold water to stop the cooking; pat dry. Separate the 4-inch pieces from the remainder of the asparagus.

Reduce the oven temperature to 375°F. Place the tart pan in a foil-lined, shallow baking pan. Scatter the 1-inch pieces of asparagus on the bottom of the crust; top with the chicken pieces. Sprinkle evenly with the Gruyère, Parmesan, and chives. Whisk the eggs together to blend; whisk in the cream, milk, salt, pepper, and nutmeg. Pour slowly into the tart pan. Arrange the reserved 4-inch asparagus spears in a spoke pattern around the top. Bake for 30 to 35 minutes, until browned and slightly puffed, and a knife inserted in the center comes out clean.

TRUC:

PREBAKING THE CRUST KEEPS THE BOTTOM FROM GETTING SOGGY. WHEN THE DOUGH IS LINED WITH ALUMINUM FOIL AND WEIGHTS, THE CRUST KEEPS ITS SHAPE WHILE BAKING AND DOESN'T BUBBLE UP. THIS PROCESS IS SOMETIMES CALLED "BAKING BLIND."

RESOURCES

ADRIANA'S CARAVAN
www.adrianascaravan.com
1–800–316–0820
Couscous
Herbes de Provence
Lavender
Preserved lemon
Ras el hanout
Sherry vinegar
Sweet Spanish paprika

CHEFSHOP.COM
www.chefshop.com
1–877–337–2491
Hazelnut oil
Herbes de Provence
Lavender honey
Piment d'Espelette
Sherry vinegar
Vinaigre de Banyuls
Walnut oil

D'ARTAGNAN
www.dartagnan.com
1–800–327–8246
Capon
Chickens
Foie gras
Poussins

GRANDFOOD.COM
www.grandfood.com
Aged wine vinegar
Sherry vinegar
Verjus

JOIE DE VIVRE
www.frenchselections.com
1–800–648–8854
Dried cèpes
Dried morels
Foie gras
Harissa
Herbes de Provence
Lavender honey
Niçoise olives
Old wine vinegar
Walnut oil

PENZEYS SPICES
www.penzeys.com
1–800–741–7787
Herbes de Provence
Lavender (not listed in catalogue
   but available)
Paprika
Saffron

TIENDA.COM
www.tienda.com
1–888–472–1022
Bomba Rice
Smoked Spanish paprika

INDEX

Curried Chicken Clafouti, 194–95
Eggnog, 198–99
Flan with Chicken Livers, 22–23
French Deviled Eggs, 204–5
Jam Omelet, 208–9
Layered Provençal Omelet, 196–97
Oven-Baked Omelet, 210–11
Shirred Eggs, 200–1
Spinach and Mushroom Quiche, 216–17
Wild Mushroom Omelet, 212–13

Fennel
    Chicken Bouillabaisse, 156–57
First courses, 12–53
Flan with Chicken Livers, 22–23
Foie gras, Boneless Chicken Breasts Stuffed with,
    70–71
French Deviled Eggs, 204–5
French terms defined, 8–9

Garbanzo beans
    Chicken Couscous, 158–59
Garlic
    Chicken with Garlic, 120–21
    Chicken with Garlic Croutons, 124–25
    Chicken and Garlic Soup, 48–49
Ginger, Low-Fat Chicken Fricassee with, 172–73
Goat cheese
    Boneless Chicken Breasts Stuffed with Goat
        Cheese and Basil, 66–67
    Chicken and Watercress Salad, 38–39
Greens. *See also specific kinds*
    Bistro Salad, 192–93
    Chicken, Corn, and Tomato Salad, 32–33
    Chicken Livers on Greens with Pan Juices, 34–35
    Chicken Salad with Grape Tendrils, 44–45
    Smoked Tea–Poached Chicken, 36–37
Grilled Chicken with Herbes de Provence, 104–5

Ham
    Basque Open-Faced Omelet, 214–15
    Basque-Style Boneless Chicken Breasts, 58–59
    Catalan Chicken, 94–95
    Country-Style Omelet, 206–7
Herbes de Provence
    Chicken Breasts with Honey, Lavender, and Herbs,
        144–45
    Grilled Chicken with Herbes de Provence, 104–5
Herbs. *See also specific kinds*
    Chicken with Chermoula, 82–83
    Vietnamese Chicken and Rice Noodle Salad, 46–47
Honey, Lavender, and Herbs, Chicken Breasts with,
    144–45

Jam Omelet, 208–9
Juniper berries
    Chicken with Ale, 162–63
    Chicken with Juniper Berries, 126–27
    Chicken with Lentils, 128–29

Lavender, and Herbs, Chicken Breasts with Honey,
    144–45
Layered Provençal Omelet, 196–97
Leeks. *See also* Vegetables
    Chicken in a Pot, 178–79
Lemons, Preserved, and Olives, Moroccan Chicken
    with, 174–75
Lentils, Chicken with, 128–29
Lettuce
    Bistro Salad, 192–93
    Chicken, Apple, Hazelnut, and Fourme d'Ambert
        Salad, 42–43
    Chicken, Pear, Roquefort, and Walnut Salad,
        40–41
    Chicken with Garlic Croutons, 124–25
    Chicken and Watercress Salad, 38–39
    Curried Chicken Salad Sampler, 30–31